HUMANITIES
HEALTH
BIOLOGY
Economics
SOCIOLOGY
CALCULUS
LITERATURE
Grammar
ANATOMY
PHYSICS
World History

DEMETER & PERSEPHONE

SPRING HELD HOSTAGE

A GREEK MYTH

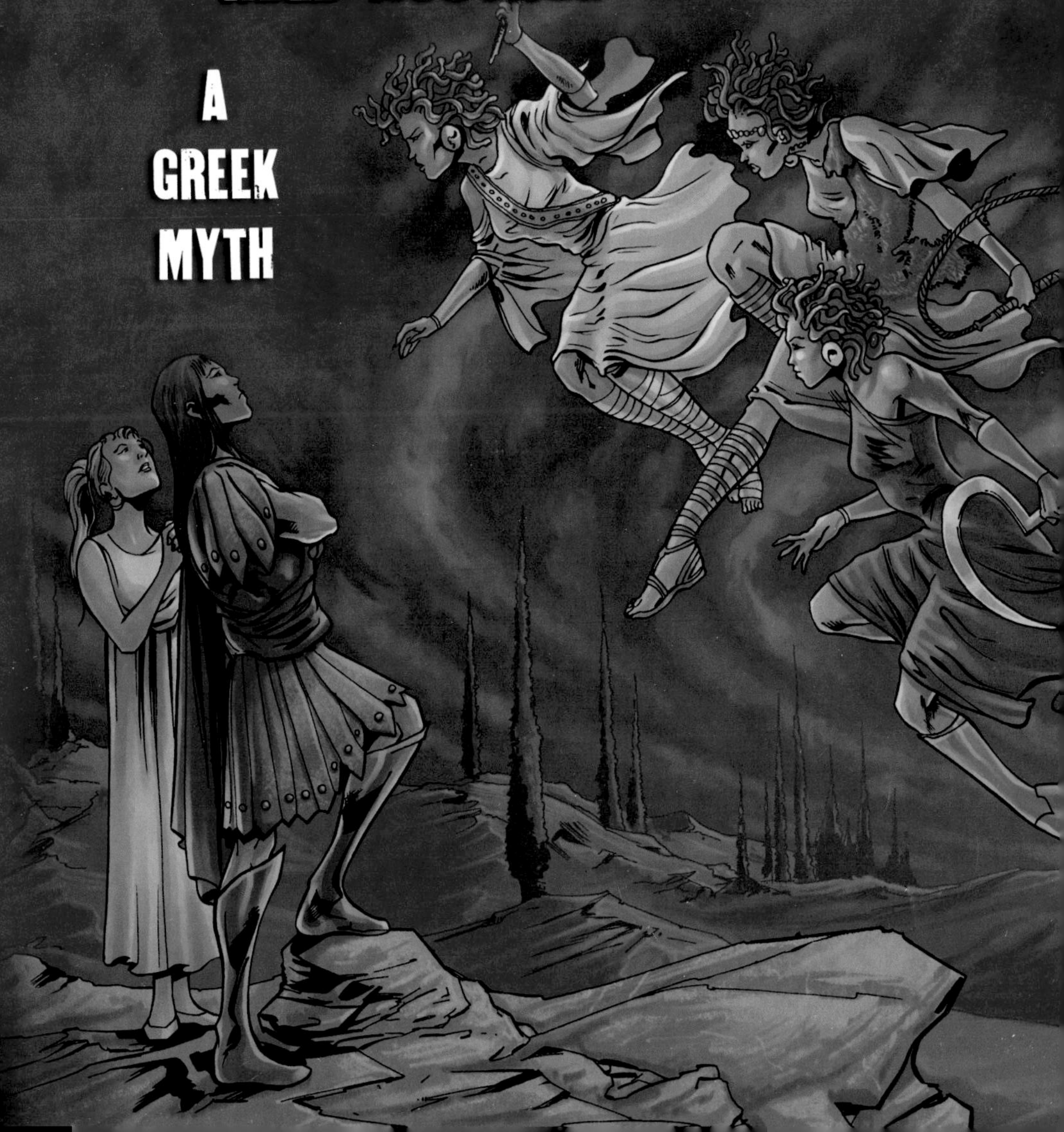

STORY BY
JUSTINE & RON FONTES

PENCILS BY
STEVE KURTH

INKS BY
BARBARA SCHULZ

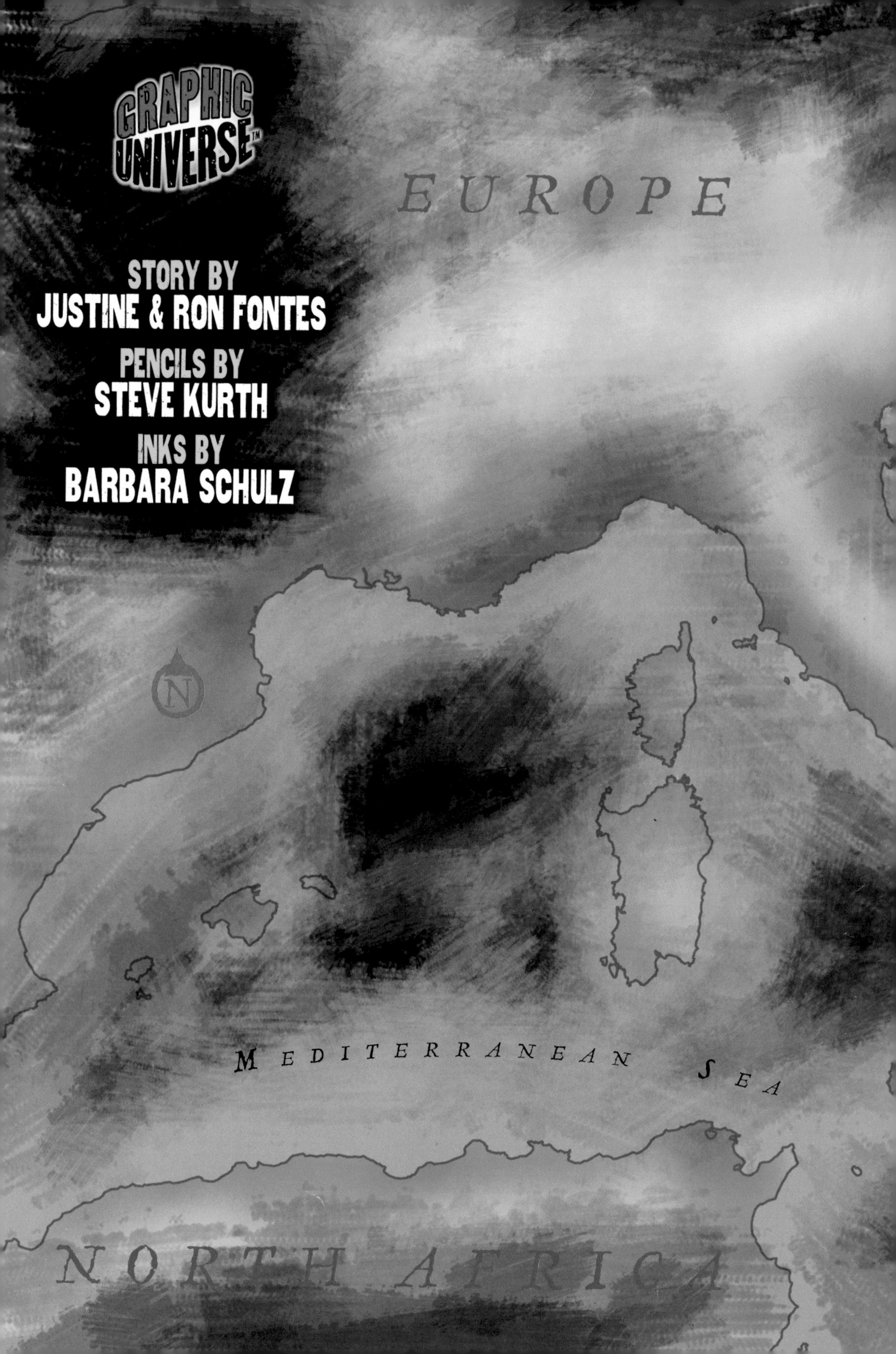
EUROPE
N
MEDITERRANEAN SEA
NORTH AFRICA

DEMETER & PERSEPHONE

SPRING HELD HOSTAGE

A GREEK MYTH

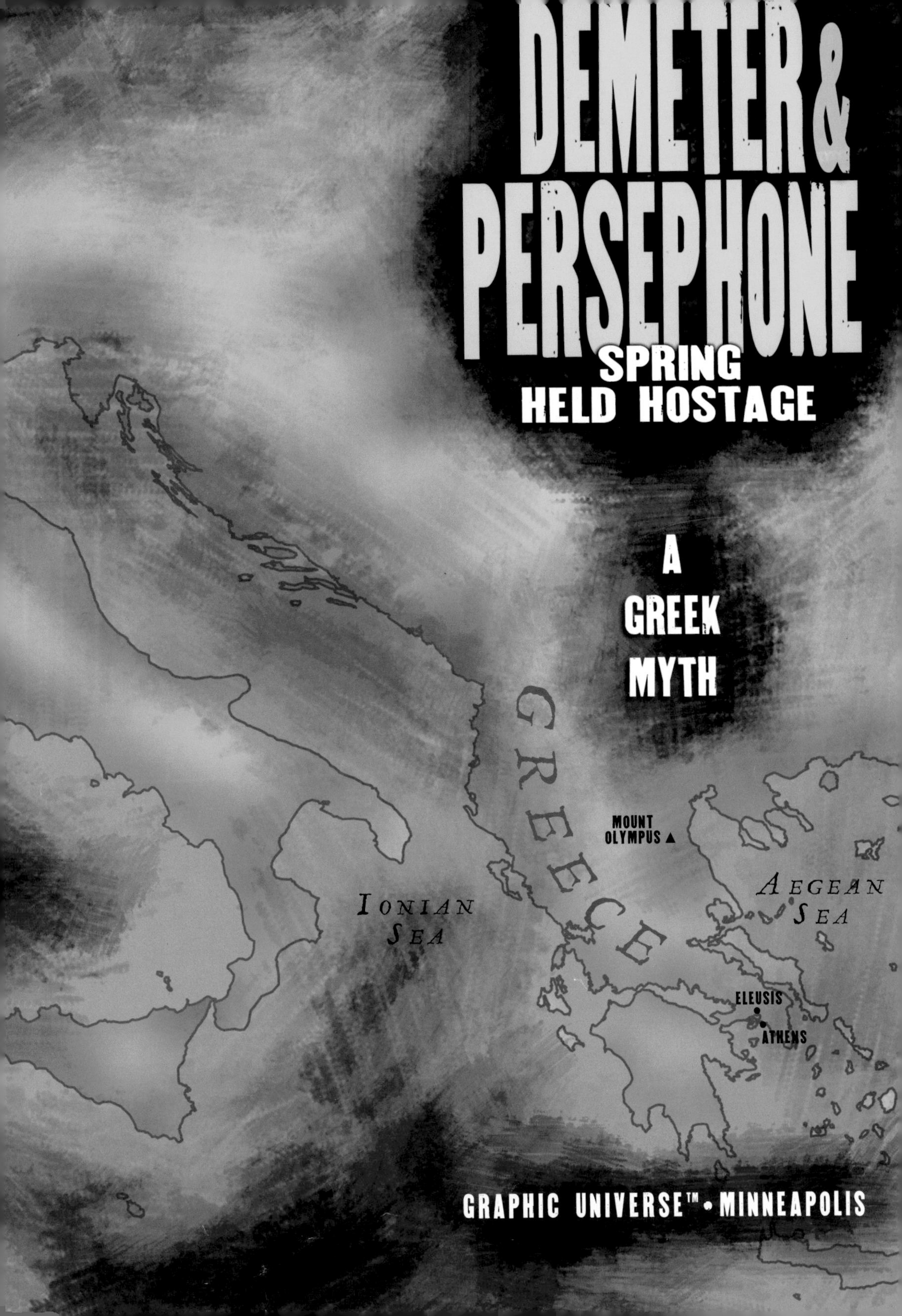
GREECE
MOUNT OLYMPUS
AEGEAN SEA
IONIAN SEA
ELEUSIS
ATHENS

GRAPHIC UNIVERSE™ • MINNEAPOLIS

Demeter is one of the most important figures in Greek mythology. She is the goddess of farming (especially corn and grains) and of the harvest. For the ancient Greeks, the story of Demeter's search for her kidnapped daughter Persephone explains the cycle of seasons. Persephone's reunion with her mother represents the beginning of springtime—the return of warm weather and budding crops. For more than two thousand years, followers of Demeter celebrated the harvest of those crops in secret rituals at the goddess's temple in Eleusis, Greece.

In retelling Demeter's story, Justine and Ron Fontes used classical and modern sources such as Ovid's *Metamorphoses* and Edith Hamilton's *Mythology*. Artist Steve Kurth used classical Greek art and anthropological sources to create the visual details. And David Mulroy of the University of Wisconsin-Milwaukee ensured historical and visual accuracy.

STORY BY JUSTINE AND RON FONTES

PENCILS BY STEVE KURTH

INKS BY BARBARA SCHULZ

COLORING AND LETTERING BY RAY DILLON OF GOLDEN GOAT STUDIOS

CONSULTANT: DAVID MULROY, UNIVERSITY OF WISCONSIN-MILWAUKEE

Copyright © 2007 by Lerner Publications Company

Graphic Universe™ is a trademark of Lerner Publications Company.

Graphic Universe ™
An imprint of Lerner Publishing Group
241 First Avenue North
Minneapolis, MN 55401 U.S.A.

Website address: www.lernerbooks.com

Library of Congress Cataloging-in-Publication Data

Fontes, Justine.
    Demeter and Persephone : spring held hostage / story by Justine and Ron Fontes ; pencils by Steve Kurth ; inks by Barbara Schulz.
        p. cm. — (Graphic myths and legends)
    Includes index.
        ISBN-13: 978-0-8225-5966-5 (lib. bdg. : alk. paper)
        ISBN-10: 0-8225-5966-8 (lib. bdg. : alk. paper)
        1. Demeter (Greek deity)—Juvenile literature.
    2. Persephone (Greek deity)—Juvenile literature.
    I. Fontes, Ron. II. Kurth, Steve. III. Schulz, Barbara Jo. IV. Title. V. Series.
    BL820.C5F66 2007
    741.5'973—dc22   2006006769

Manufactured in the United States of America
1 2 3 4 5 6 - JR - 12 11 10 09 08 07

TABLE OF CONTENTS

A WINTERLESS WORLD

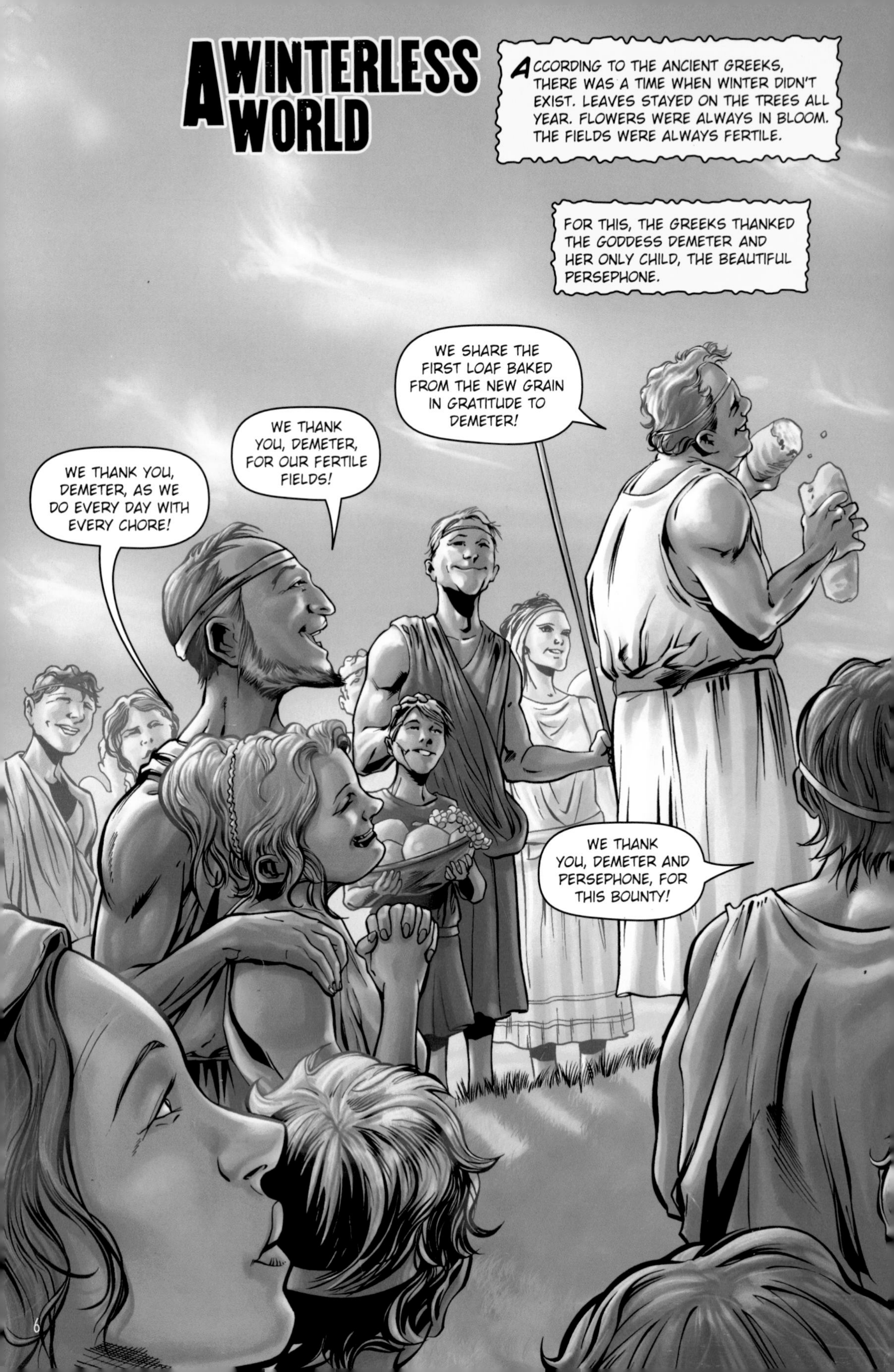
ACCORDING TO THE ANCIENT GREEKS, THERE WAS A TIME WHEN WINTER DIDN'T EXIST. LEAVES STAYED ON THE TREES ALL YEAR. FLOWERS WERE ALWAYS IN BLOOM. THE FIELDS WERE ALWAYS FERTILE.
FOR THIS, THE GREEKS THANKED THE GODDESS DEMETER AND HER ONLY CHILD, THE BEAUTIFUL PERSEPHONE.
WE THANK YOU, DEMETER, AS WE DO EVERY DAY WITH EVERY CHORE!
WE THANK YOU, DEMETER, FOR OUR FERTILE FIELDS!
WE SHARE THE FIRST LOAF BAKED FROM THE NEW GRAIN IN GRATITUDE TO DEMETER!
WE THANK YOU, DEMETER AND PERSEPHONE, FOR THIS BOUNTY!

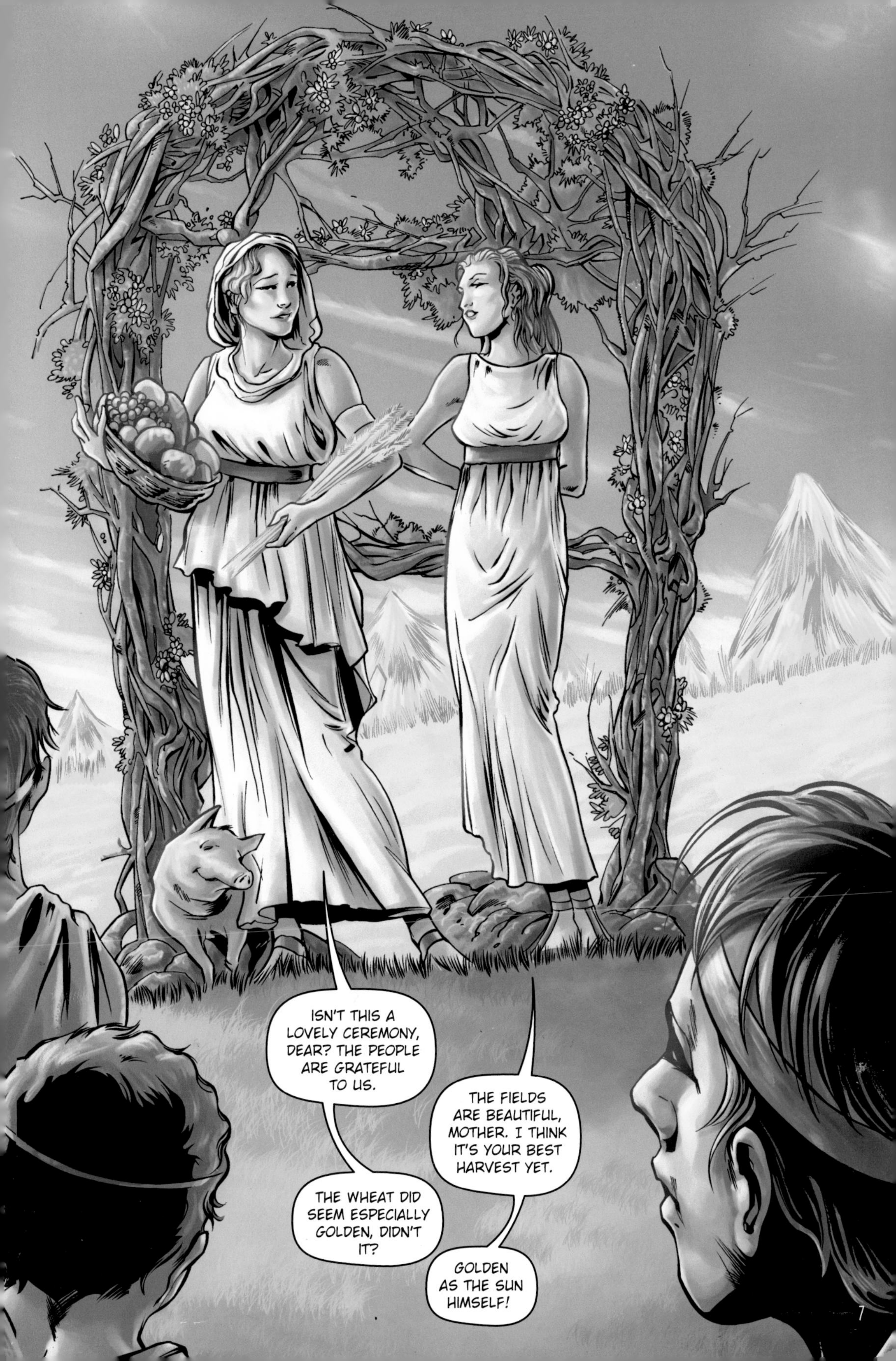
ISN'T THIS A LOVELY CEREMONY, DEAR? THE PEOPLE ARE GRATEFUL TO US.
THE FIELDS ARE BEAUTIFUL, MOTHER. I THINK IT'S YOUR BEST HARVEST YET.
THE WHEAT DID SEEM ESPECIALLY GOLDEN, DIDN'T IT?
GOLDEN AS THE SUN HIMSELF!

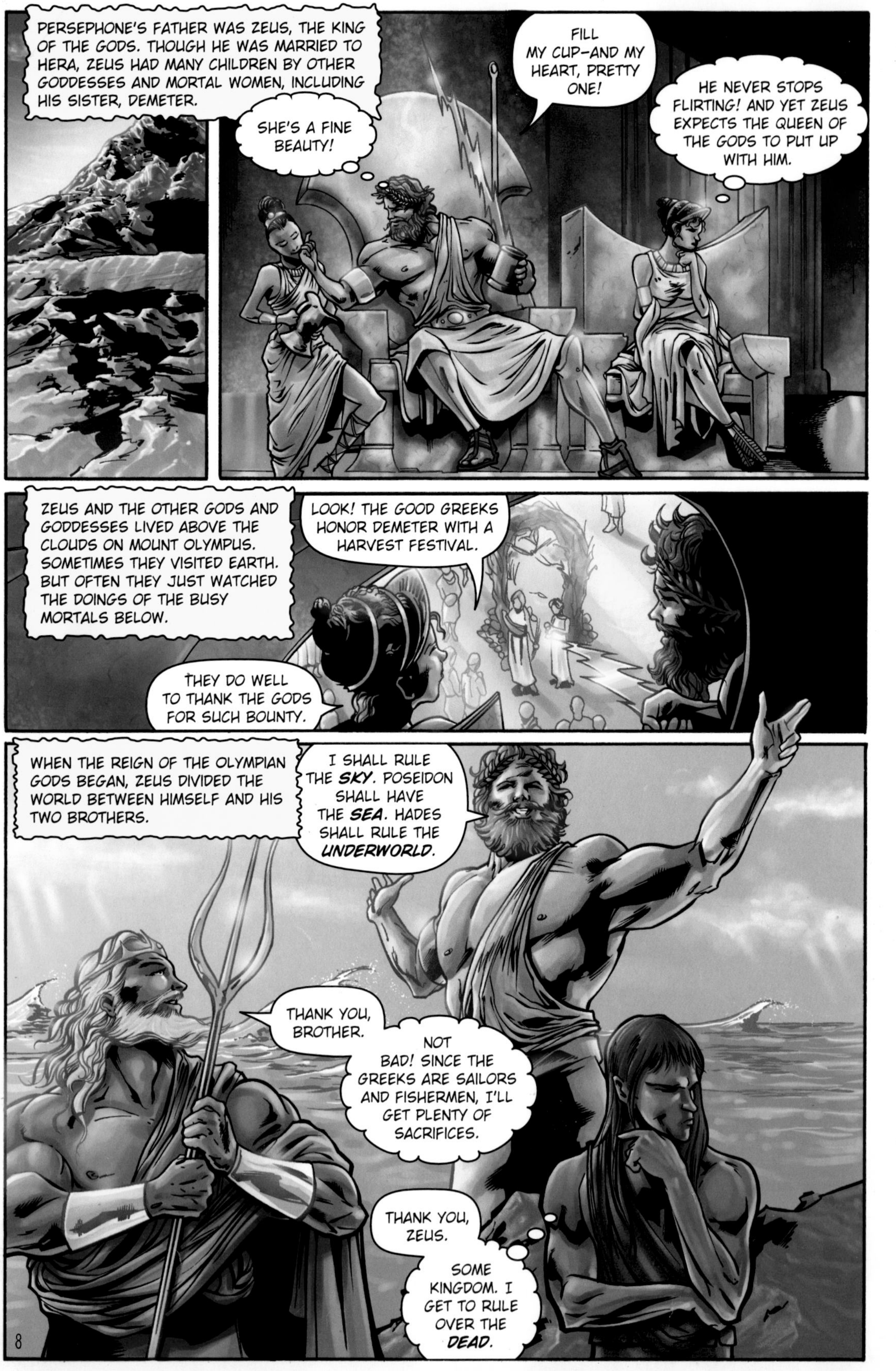
PERSEPHONE'S FATHER WAS ZEUS, THE KING OF THE GODS. THOUGH HE WAS MARRIED TO HERA, ZEUS HAD MANY CHILDREN BY OTHER GODDESSES AND MORTAL WOMEN, INCLUDING HIS SISTER, DEMETER.
SHE'S A FINE BEAUTY!
FILL MY CUP—AND MY HEART, PRETTY ONE!
HE NEVER STOPS FLIRTING! AND YET ZEUS EXPECTS THE QUEEN OF THE GODS TO PUT UP WITH HIM.
ZEUS AND THE OTHER GODS AND GODDESSES LIVED ABOVE THE CLOUDS ON MOUNT OLYMPUS. SOMETIMES THEY VISITED EARTH. BUT OFTEN THEY JUST WATCHED THE DOINGS OF THE BUSY MORTALS BELOW.
LOOK! THE GOOD GREEKS HONOR DEMETER WITH A HARVEST FESTIVAL.
THEY DO WELL TO THANK THE GODS FOR SUCH BOUNTY.
WHEN THE REIGN OF THE OLYMPIAN GODS BEGAN, ZEUS DIVIDED THE WORLD BETWEEN HIMSELF AND HIS TWO BROTHERS.
I SHALL RULE THE ***SKY***. POSEIDON SHALL HAVE THE ***SEA***. HADES SHALL RULE THE ***UNDERWORLD***.
THANK YOU, BROTHER.
NOT BAD! SINCE THE GREEKS ARE SAILORS AND FISHERMEN, I'LL GET PLENTY OF SACRIFICES.
THANK YOU, ZEUS.
SOME KINGDOM. I GET TO RULE OVER THE ***DEAD***.

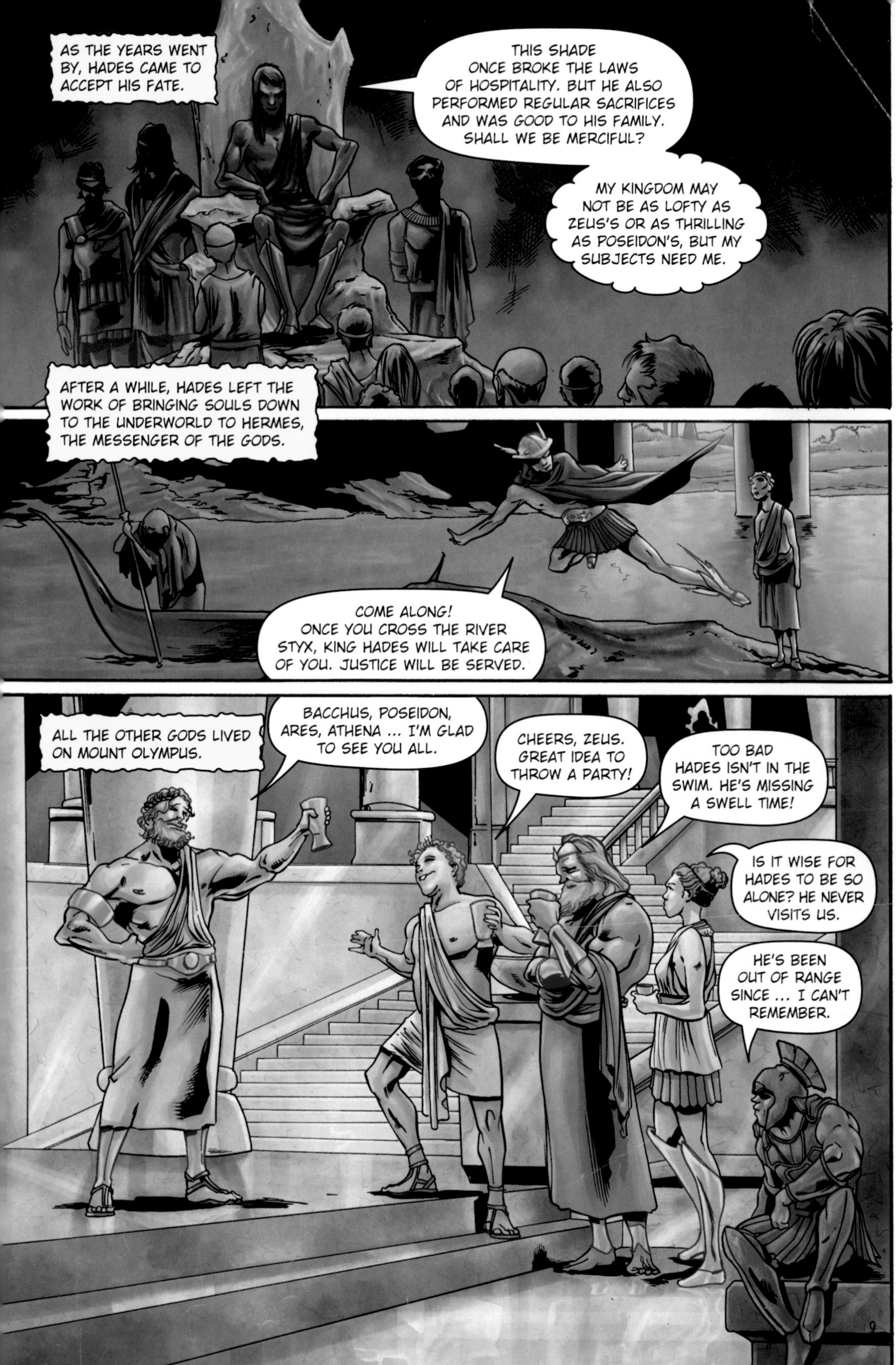
AS THE YEARS WENT BY, HADES CAME TO ACCEPT HIS FATE.
THIS SHADE ONCE BROKE THE LAWS OF HOSPITALITY. BUT HE ALSO PERFORMED REGULAR SACRIFICES AND WAS GOOD TO HIS FAMILY. SHALL WE BE MERCIFUL?
MY KINGDOM MAY NOT BE AS LOFTY AS ZEUS'S OR AS THRILLING AS POSEIDON'S, BUT MY SUBJECTS NEED ME.
AFTER A WHILE, HADES LEFT THE WORK OF BRINGING SOULS DOWN TO THE UNDERWORLD TO HERMES, THE MESSENGER OF THE GODS.
COME ALONG! ONCE YOU CROSS THE RIVER STYX, KING HADES WILL TAKE CARE OF YOU. JUSTICE WILL BE SERVED.
ALL THE OTHER GODS LIVED ON MOUNT OLYMPUS.
BACCHUS, POSEIDON, ARES, ATHENA ... I'M GLAD TO SEE YOU ALL.
CHEERS, ZEUS. GREAT IDEA TO THROW A PARTY!
TOO BAD HADES ISN'T IN THE SWIM. HE'S MISSING A SWELL TIME!
IS IT WISE FOR HADES TO BE SO ALONE? HE NEVER VISITS US.
HE'S BEEN OUT OF RANGE SINCE ... I CAN'T REMEMBER.

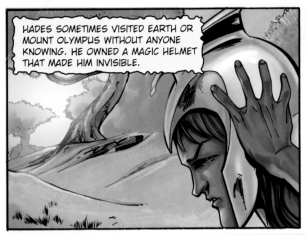

HADES SOMETIMES VISITED EARTH OR MOUNT OLYMPUS WITHOUT ANYONE KNOWING. HE OWNED A MAGIC HELMET THAT MADE HIM INVISIBLE.

A HANDY HAT INDEED!

NOW I CAN WATCH MY FAVORITE MAIDEN AT PLAY. AH, *PERSEPHONE*! SHE IS MORE BEAUTIFUL THAN EVERY FLOWER IN THIS SUNNY MEADOW.

ONE DAY, ZEUS VISITED HADES IN HIS UNDERGROUND PALACE.

SO, BROTHER, HOW ARE THINGS ON MOUNT OLYMPUS?

JUST FINE, EXCEPT THAT EVERYONE MISSES YOU.

MY MANY DUTIES KEEP ME BUSY. BUT I HAVE ALSO GROWN ACCUSTOMED TO THE UNDERWORLD.

THEN YOU ARE HAPPY?

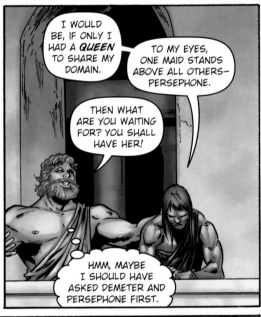

I WOULD BE, IF ONLY I HAD A *QUEEN* TO SHARE MY DOMAIN.

TO MY EYES, ONE MAID STANDS ABOVE ALL OTHERS— PERSEPHONE.

THEN WHAT ARE YOU WAITING FOR? YOU SHALL HAVE HER!

HMM, MAYBE I SHOULD HAVE ASKED DEMETER AND PERSEPHONE FIRST.

THANKS, ZEUS! YOU'RE THE GREATEST.

YES, WELL, GOOD LUCK WITH THAT.

IF I TELL DEMETER NOW, THERE'LL BE ALL KINDS OF *TROUBLE*. IF I JUST LET THINGS RUN THEIR COURSE ...

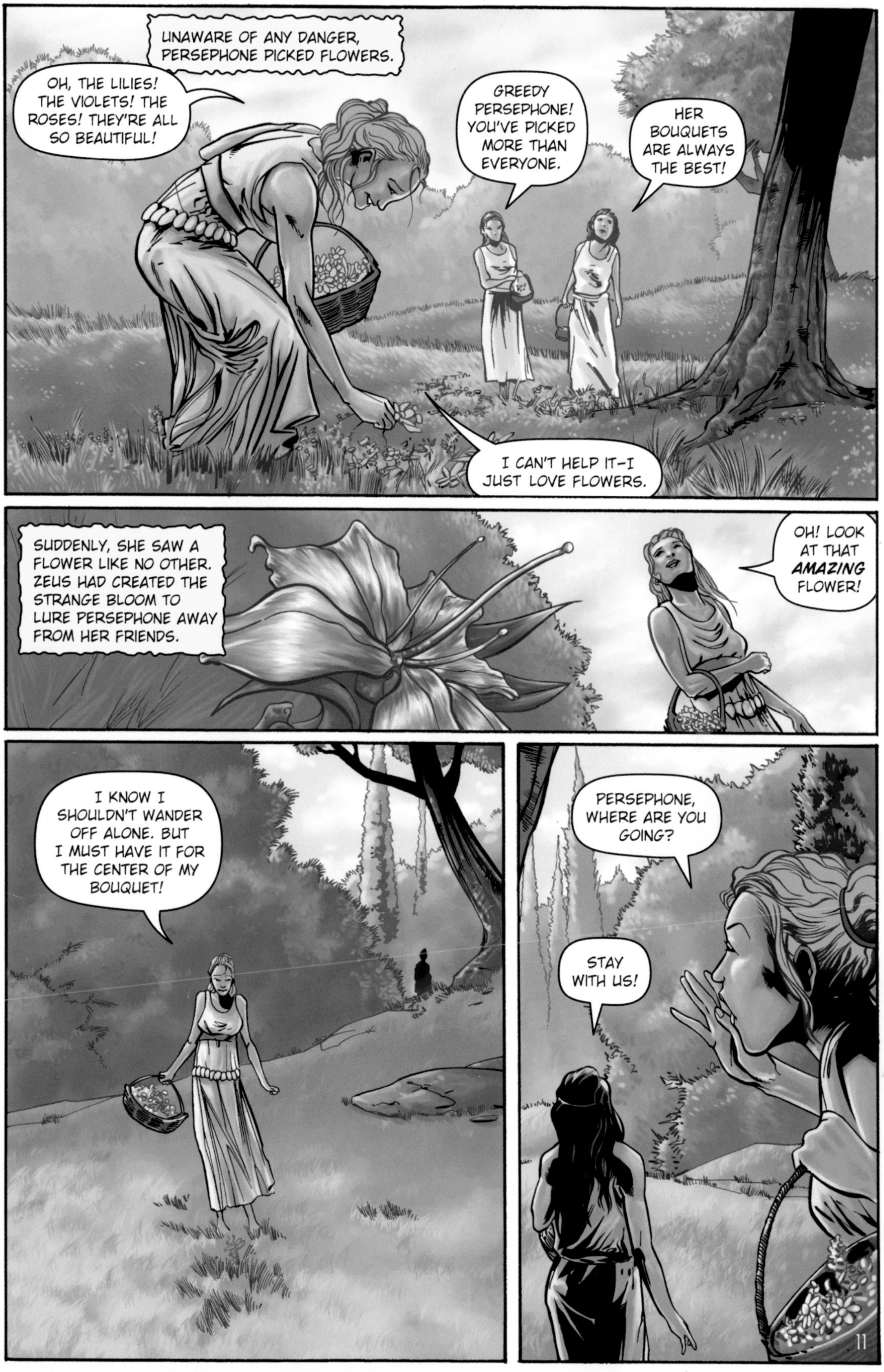

UNAWARE OF ANY DANGER, PERSEPHONE PICKED FLOWERS.
OH, THE LILIES! THE VIOLETS! THE ROSES! THEY'RE ALL SO BEAUTIFUL!
GREEDY PERSEPHONE! YOU'VE PICKED MORE THAN EVERYONE.
HER BOUQUETS ARE ALWAYS THE BEST!
I CAN'T HELP IT—I JUST LOVE FLOWERS.
SUDDENLY, SHE SAW A FLOWER LIKE NO OTHER. ZEUS HAD CREATED THE STRANGE BLOOM TO LURE PERSEPHONE AWAY FROM HER FRIENDS.
OH! LOOK AT THAT **AMAZING** FLOWER!
I KNOW I SHOULDN'T WANDER OFF ALONE. BUT I MUST HAVE IT FOR THE CENTER OF MY BOUQUET!
PERSEPHONE, WHERE ARE YOU GOING?
STAY WITH US!

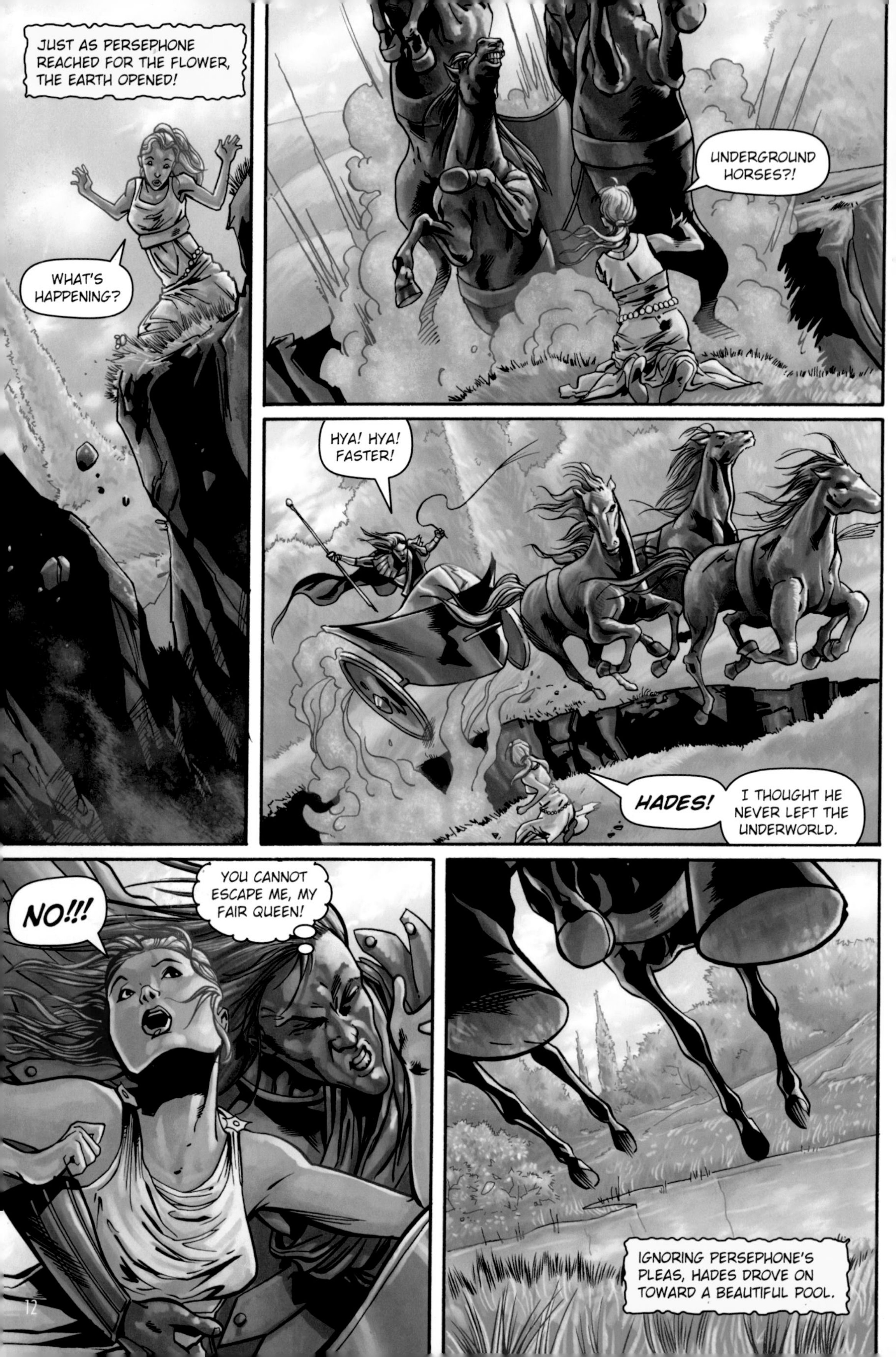
JUST AS PERSEPHONE REACHED FOR THE FLOWER, THE EARTH OPENED!
WHAT'S HAPPENING?
UNDERGROUND HORSES?!
HYA! HYA! FASTER!
HADES!
I THOUGHT HE NEVER LEFT THE UNDERWORLD.
NO!!!
YOU CANNOT ESCAPE ME, MY FAIR QUEEN!
IGNORING PERSEPHONE'S PLEAS, HADES DROVE ON TOWARD A BEAUTIFUL POOL.

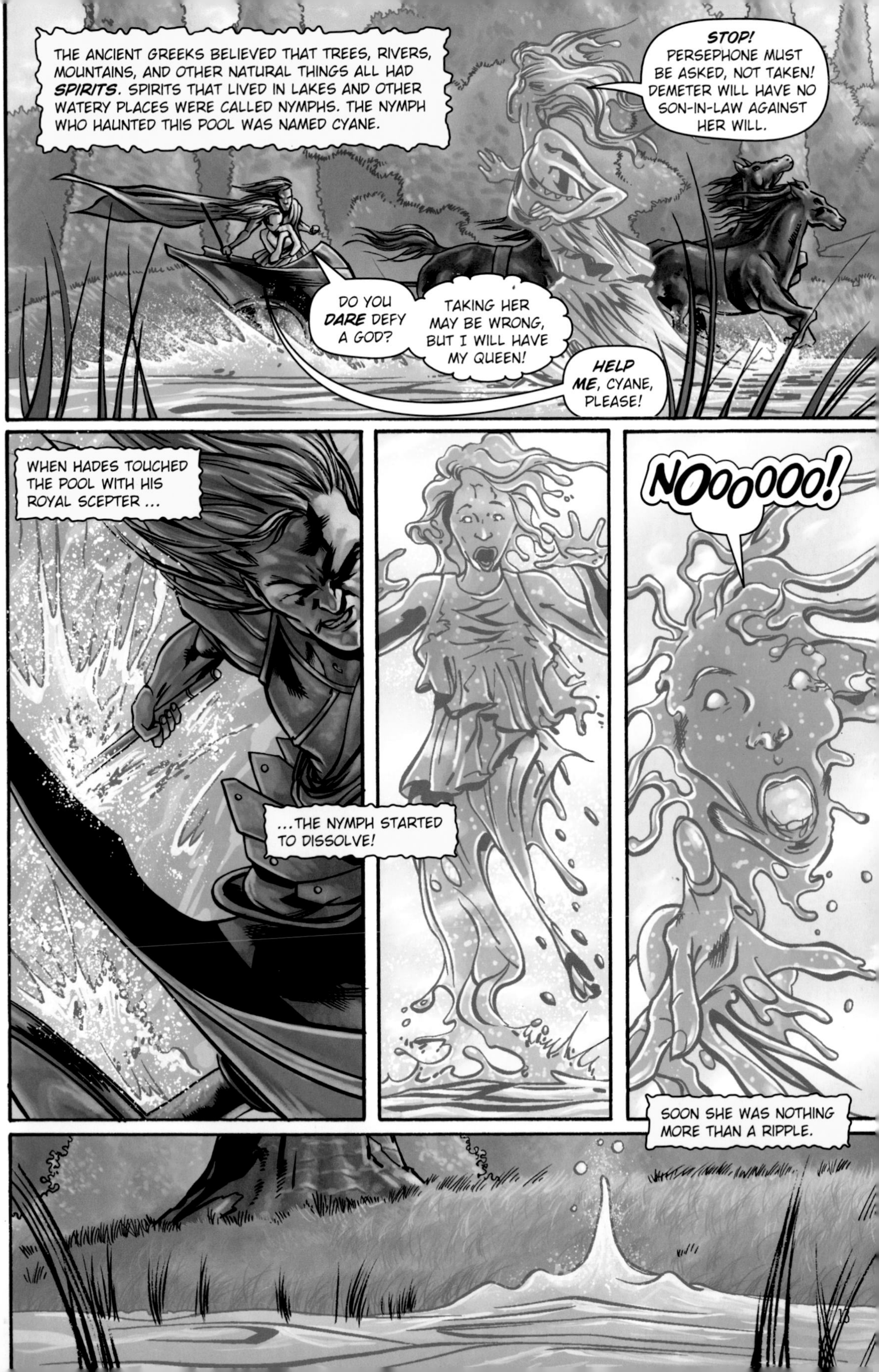
THE ANCIENT GREEKS BELIEVED THAT TREES, RIVERS, MOUNTAINS, AND OTHER NATURAL THINGS ALL HAD SPIRITS. SPIRITS THAT LIVED IN LAKES AND OTHER WATERY PLACES WERE CALLED NYMPHS. THE NYMPH WHO HAUNTED THIS POOL WAS NAMED CYANE.
STOP! PERSEPHONE MUST BE ASKED, NOT TAKEN! DEMETER WILL HAVE NO SON-IN-LAW AGAINST HER WILL.
DO YOU DARE DEFY A GOD?
TAKING HER MAY BE WRONG, BUT I WILL HAVE MY QUEEN!
HELP ME, CYANE, PLEASE!
WHEN HADES TOUCHED THE POOL WITH HIS ROYAL SCEPTER ...
...THE NYMPH STARTED TO DISSOLVE!
NOOOOOO!
SOON SHE WAS NOTHING MORE THAN A RIPPLE.

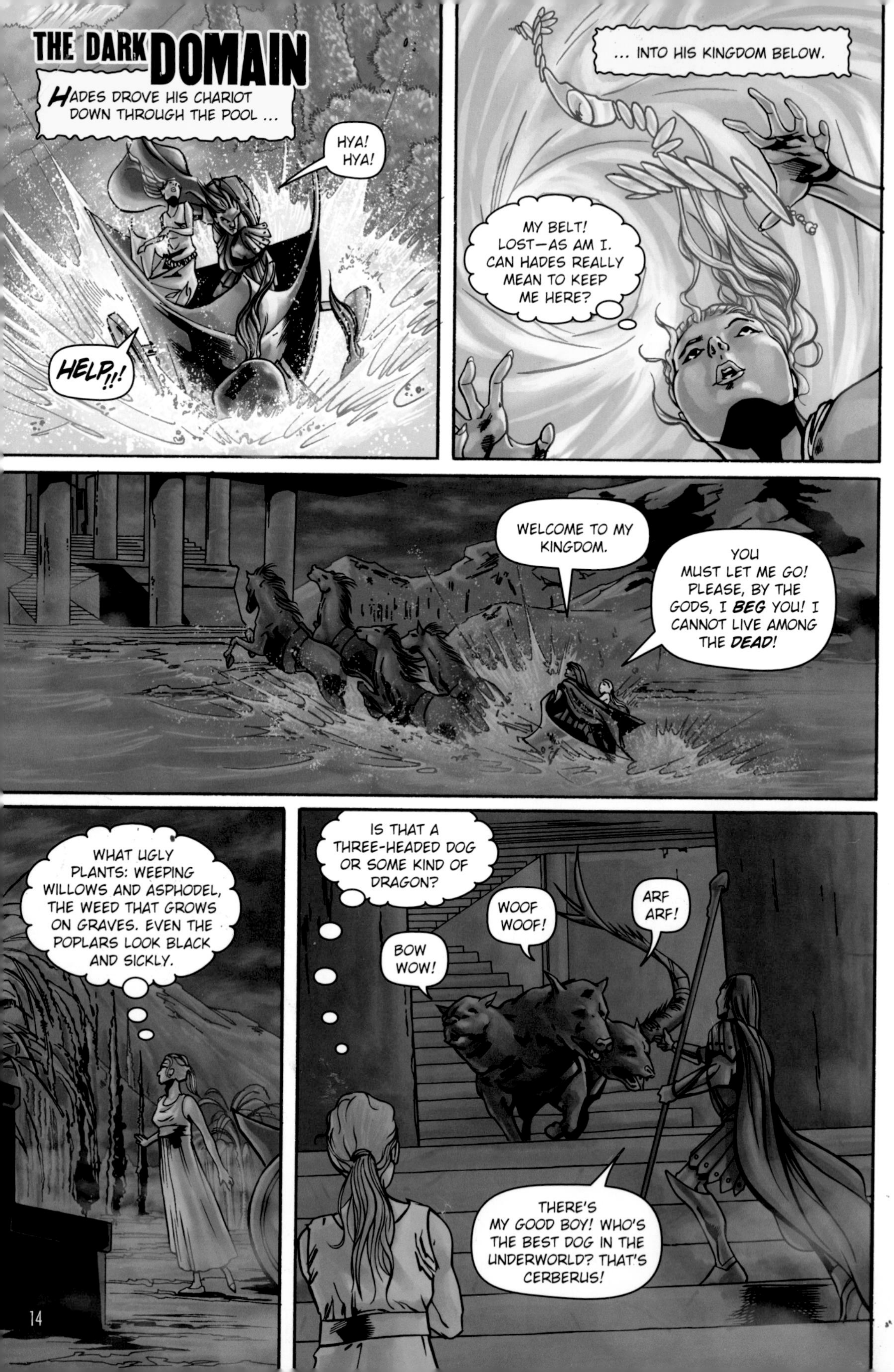
THE DARK DOMAIN
HADES DROVE HIS CHARIOT DOWN THROUGH THE POOL ...
HYA! HYA!
HELP!!!
... INTO HIS KINGDOM BELOW.
MY BELT! LOST—AS AM I. CAN HADES REALLY MEAN TO KEEP ME HERE?
WELCOME TO MY KINGDOM.
YOU MUST LET ME GO! PLEASE, BY THE GODS, I BEG YOU! I CANNOT LIVE AMONG THE DEAD!
WHAT UGLY PLANTS: WEEPING WILLOWS AND ASPHODEL, THE WEED THAT GROWS ON GRAVES. EVEN THE POPLARS LOOK BLACK AND SICKLY.
IS THAT A THREE-HEADED DOG OR SOME KIND OF DRAGON?
BOW WOW!
WOOF WOOF!
ARF ARF!
THERE'S MY GOOD BOY! WHO'S THE BEST DOG IN THE UNDERWORLD? THAT'S CERBERUS!

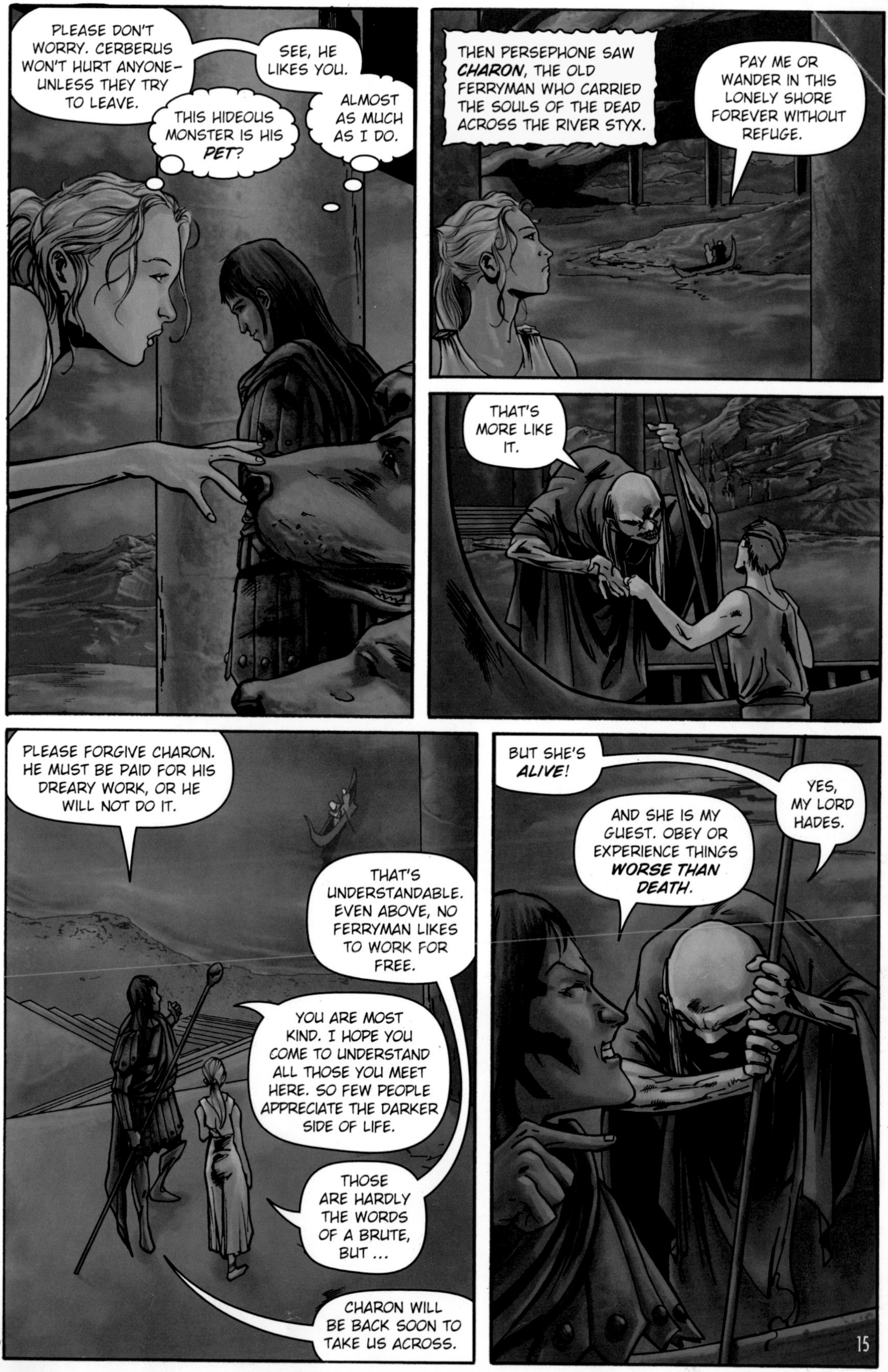
PLEASE DON'T WORRY. CERBERUS WON'T HURT ANYONE—UNLESS THEY TRY TO LEAVE.
THIS HIDEOUS MONSTER IS HIS *PET*?
SEE, HE LIKES YOU.
ALMOST AS MUCH AS I DO.
THEN PERSEPHONE SAW ***CHARON***, THE OLD FERRYMAN WHO CARRIED THE SOULS OF THE DEAD ACROSS THE RIVER STYX.
PAY ME OR WANDER IN THIS LONELY SHORE FOREVER WITHOUT REFUGE.
THAT'S MORE LIKE IT.
PLEASE FORGIVE CHARON. HE MUST BE PAID FOR HIS DREARY WORK, OR HE WILL NOT DO IT.
THAT'S UNDERSTANDABLE. EVEN ABOVE, NO FERRYMAN LIKES TO WORK FOR FREE.
YOU ARE MOST KIND. I HOPE YOU COME TO UNDERSTAND ALL THOSE YOU MEET HERE. SO FEW PEOPLE APPRECIATE THE DARKER SIDE OF LIFE.
THOSE ARE HARDLY THE WORDS OF A BRUTE, BUT ...
CHARON WILL BE BACK SOON TO TAKE US ACROSS.
BUT SHE'S ***ALIVE***!
YES, MY LORD HADES.
AND SHE IS MY GUEST. OBEY OR EXPERIENCE THINGS ***WORSE THAN DEATH***.

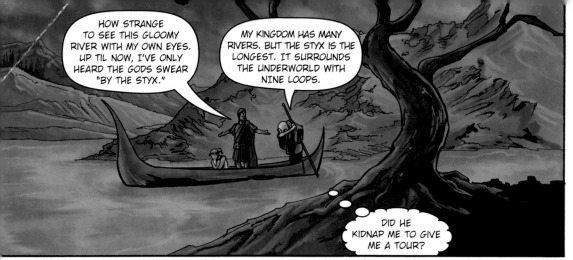

HOW STRANGE TO SEE THIS GLOOMY RIVER WITH MY OWN EYES. UP TIL NOW, I'VE ONLY HEARD THE GODS SWEAR "BY THE STYX."

MY KINGDOM HAS MANY RIVERS. BUT THE STYX IS THE LONGEST. IT SURROUNDS THE UNDERWORLD WITH NINE LOOPS.

DID HE KIDNAP ME TO GIVE ME A TOUR?

SHADES MUST CROSS THE STYX TO ENTER MY KINGDOM.

PERHAPS YOU ARE HUNGRY OR THIRSTY. MY PALACE IS NOT FAR.

OH NO! HE CAN'T TRICK ME. IF I EAT OR DRINK ANYTHING DOWN HERE, I'LL HAVE TO STAY FOREVER.

NO, THANK YOU.

SHE'LL GET HUNGRY EVENTUALLY.

I CAN BE PATIENT.

HERE ARE THE KINGS WHO HELP ME DECIDE WHETHER A SHADE GOES TO TARTARUS OR THE ELYSIAN FIELDS OR REMAINS HERE IN ACHERON.

I HAVE HEARD OF AEACUS, MINOS, AND RHADAMANTHYS. WE ARE ALL CHILDREN OF ZEUS. BUT I HAVE NEVER MET THEM BEFORE.

THEN PERHAPS YOU WOULD LIKE TO MEET THE SHADES OF SOME OF THE GREATEST MEN WHO EVER LIVED.

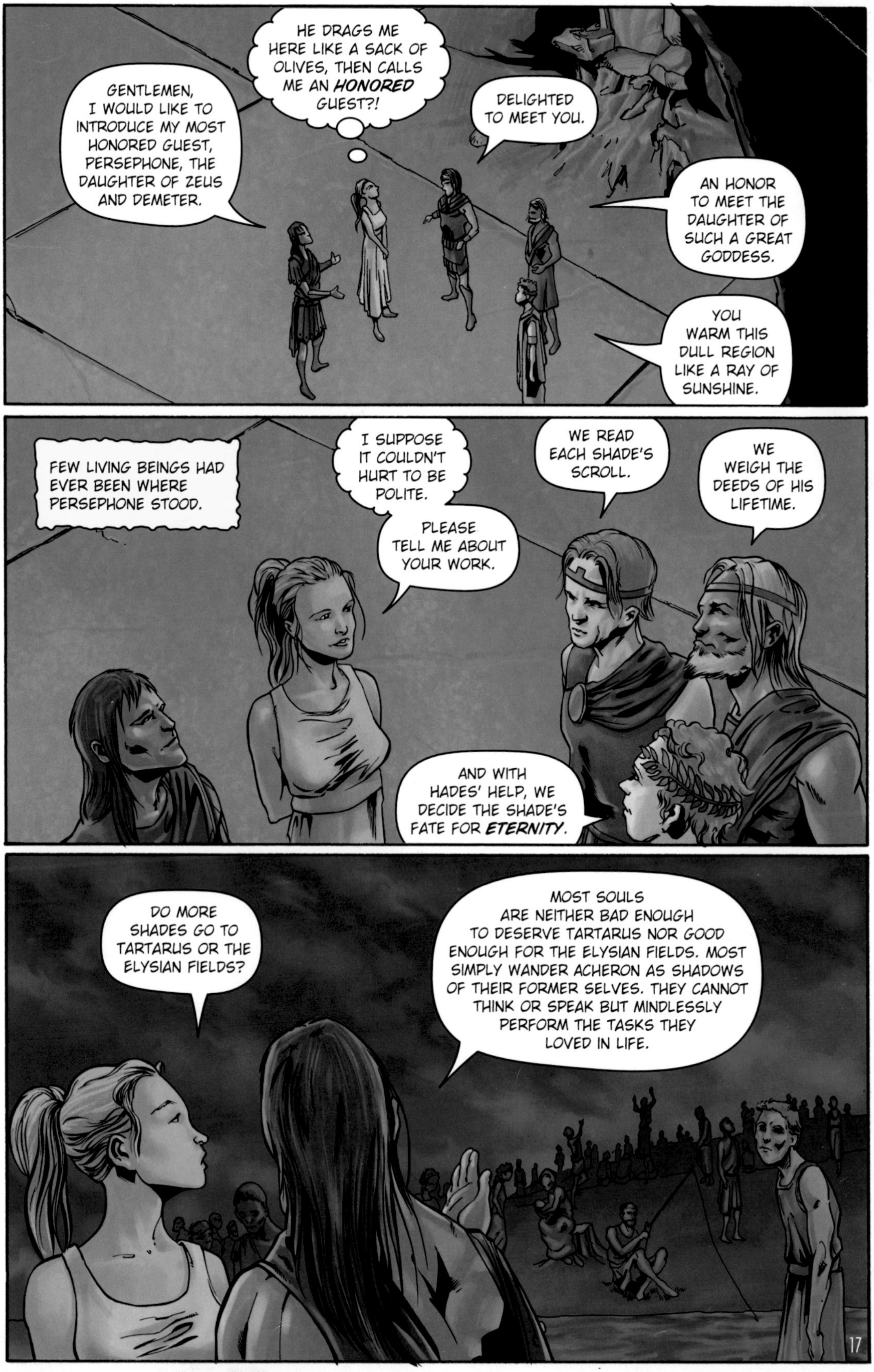

GENTLEMEN, I WOULD LIKE TO INTRODUCE MY MOST HONORED GUEST, PERSEPHONE, THE DAUGHTER OF ZEUS AND DEMETER.
HE DRAGS ME HERE LIKE A SACK OF OLIVES, THEN CALLS ME AN ***HONORED*** GUEST?!
DELIGHTED TO MEET YOU.
AN HONOR TO MEET THE DAUGHTER OF SUCH A GREAT GODDESS.
YOU WARM THIS DULL REGION LIKE A RAY OF SUNSHINE.
FEW LIVING BEINGS HAD EVER BEEN WHERE PERSEPHONE STOOD.
I SUPPOSE IT COULDN'T HURT TO BE POLITE.
PLEASE TELL ME ABOUT YOUR WORK.
WE READ EACH SHADE'S SCROLL.
WE WEIGH THE DEEDS OF HIS LIFETIME.
AND WITH HADES' HELP, WE DECIDE THE SHADE'S FATE FOR ***ETERNITY***.
DO MORE SHADES GO TO TARTARUS OR THE ELYSIAN FIELDS?
MOST SOULS ARE NEITHER BAD ENOUGH TO DESERVE TARTARUS NOR GOOD ENOUGH FOR THE ELYSIAN FIELDS. MOST SIMPLY WANDER ACHERON AS SHADOWS OF THEIR FORMER SELVES. THEY CANNOT THINK OR SPEAK BUT MINDLESSLY PERFORM THE TASKS THEY LOVED IN LIFE.

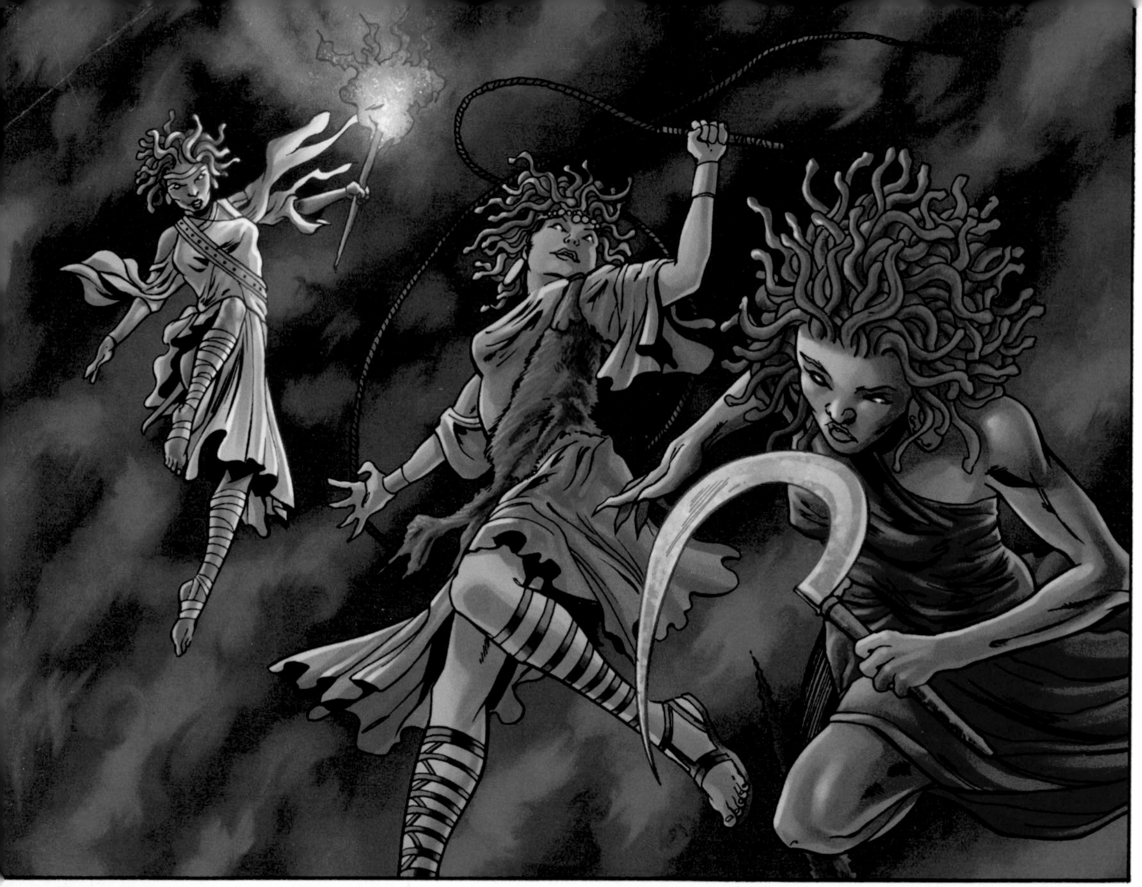

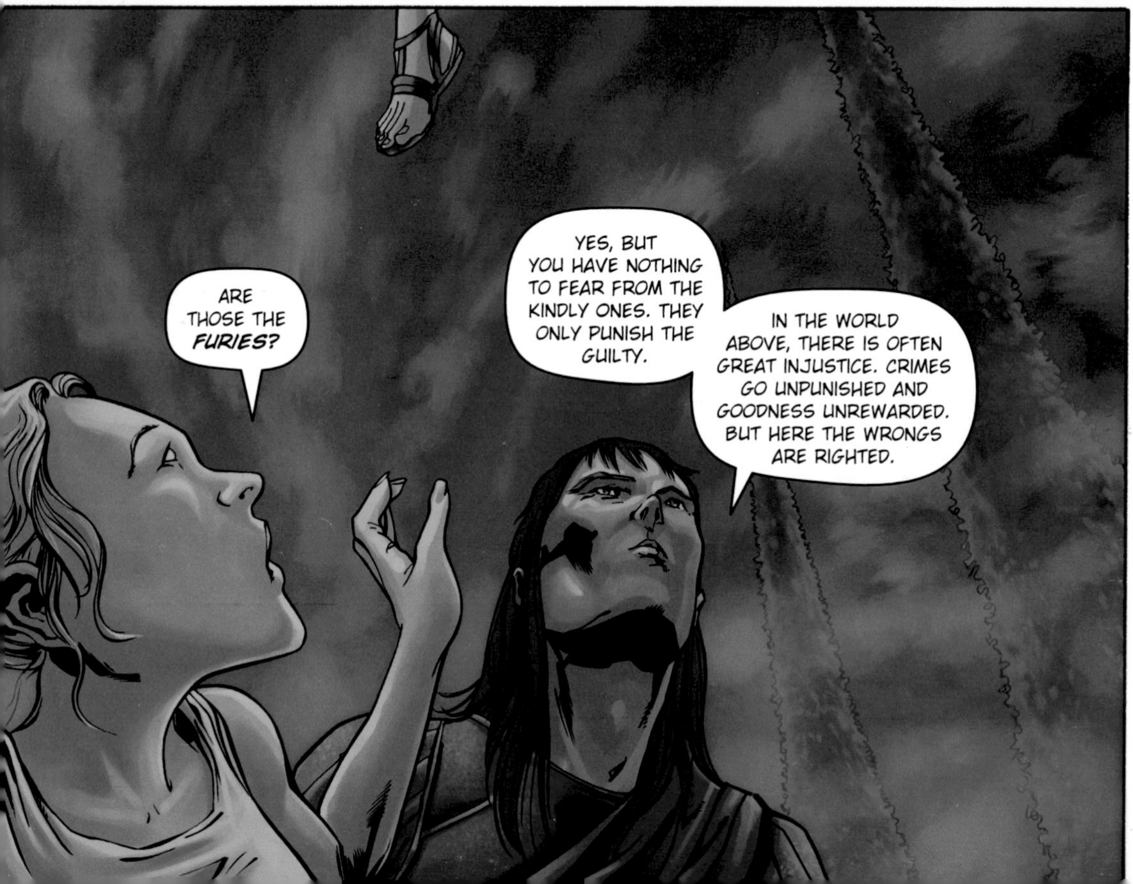
ARE THOSE THE *FURIES?*
YES, BUT YOU HAVE NOTHING TO FEAR FROM THE KINDLY ONES. THEY ONLY PUNISH THE GUILTY.
IN THE WORLD ABOVE, THERE IS OFTEN GREAT INJUSTICE. CRIMES GO UNPUNISHED AND GOODNESS UNREWARDED. BUT HERE THE WRONGS ARE RIGHTED.

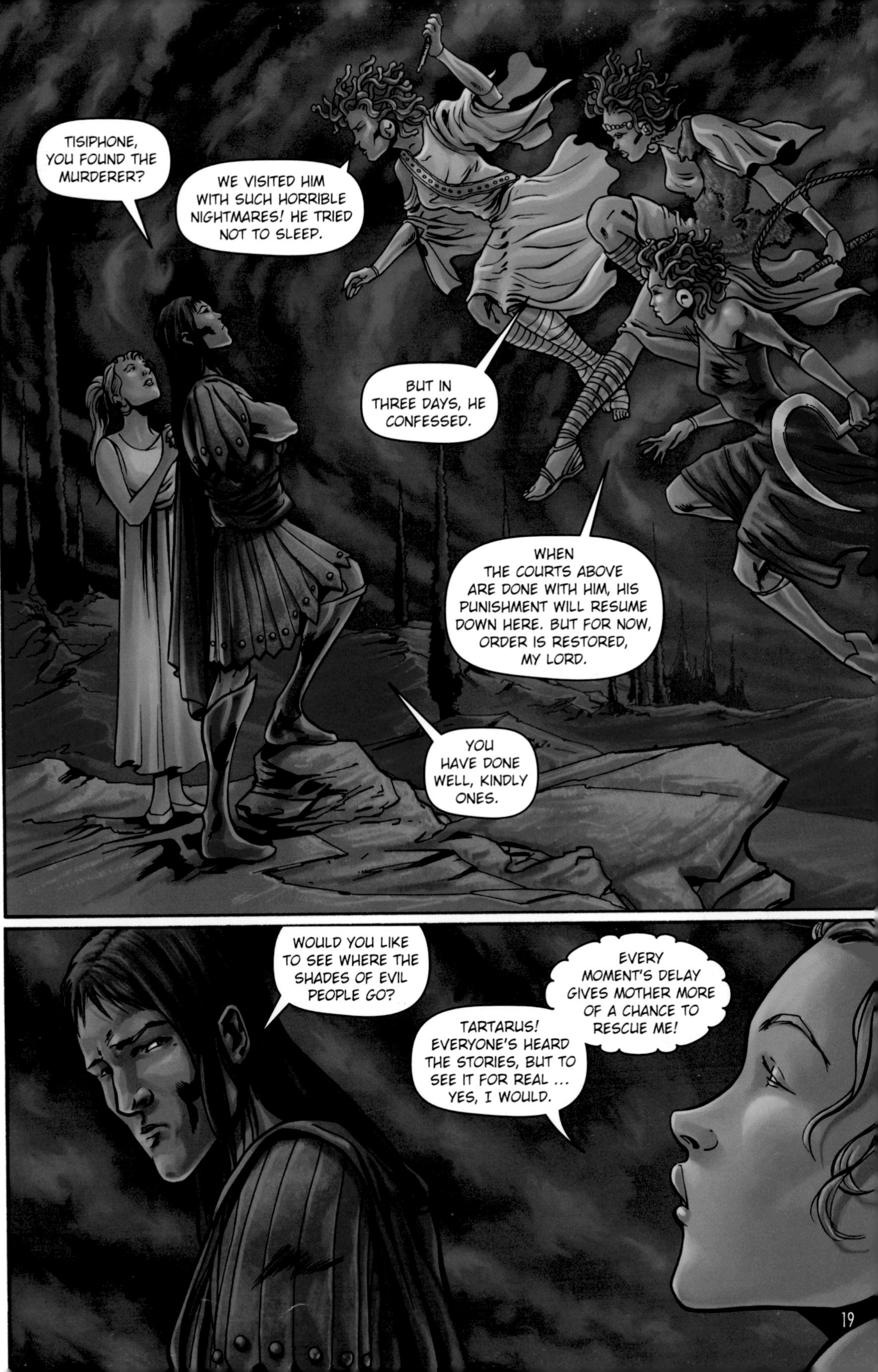
TISIPHONE, YOU FOUND THE MURDERER?
WE VISITED HIM WITH SUCH HORRIBLE NIGHTMARES! HE TRIED NOT TO SLEEP.
BUT IN THREE DAYS, HE CONFESSED.
WHEN THE COURTS ABOVE ARE DONE WITH HIM, HIS PUNISHMENT WILL RESUME DOWN HERE. BUT FOR NOW, ORDER IS RESTORED, MY LORD.
YOU HAVE DONE WELL, KINDLY ONES.
WOULD YOU LIKE TO SEE WHERE THE SHADES OF EVIL PEOPLE GO?
EVERY MOMENT'S DELAY GIVES MOTHER MORE OF A CHANCE TO RESCUE ME!
TARTARUS! EVERYONE'S HEARD THE STORIES, BUT TO SEE IT FOR REAL ... YES, I WOULD.

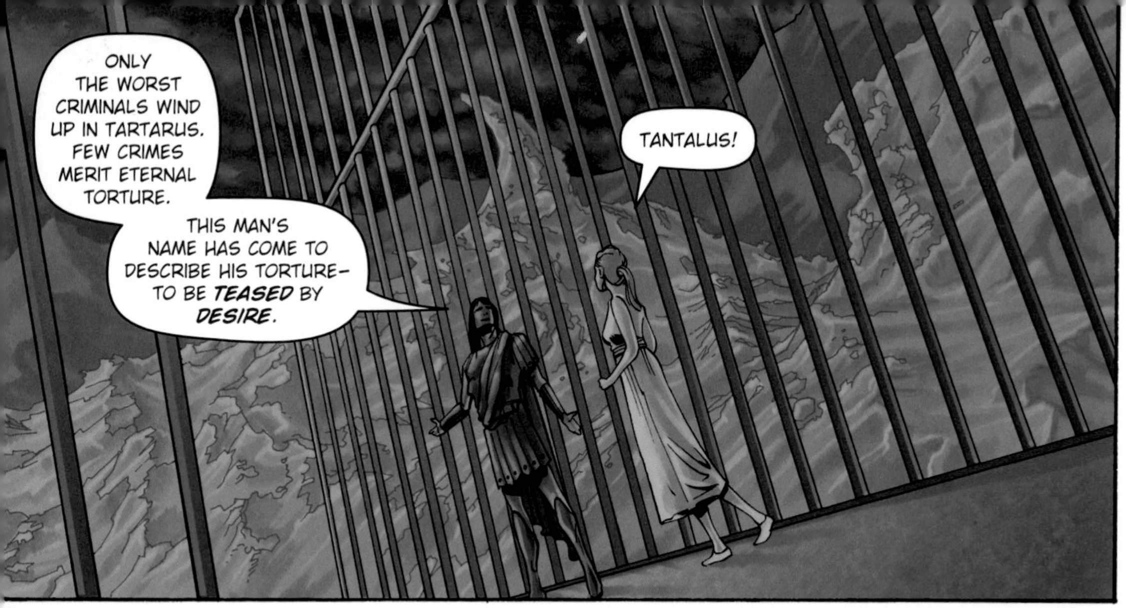
ONLY THE WORST CRIMINALS WIND UP IN TARTARUS. FEW CRIMES MERIT ETERNAL TORTURE.
THIS MAN'S NAME HAS COME TO DESCRIBE HIS TORTURE– TO BE *TEASED* BY *DESIRE*.
TANTALUS!

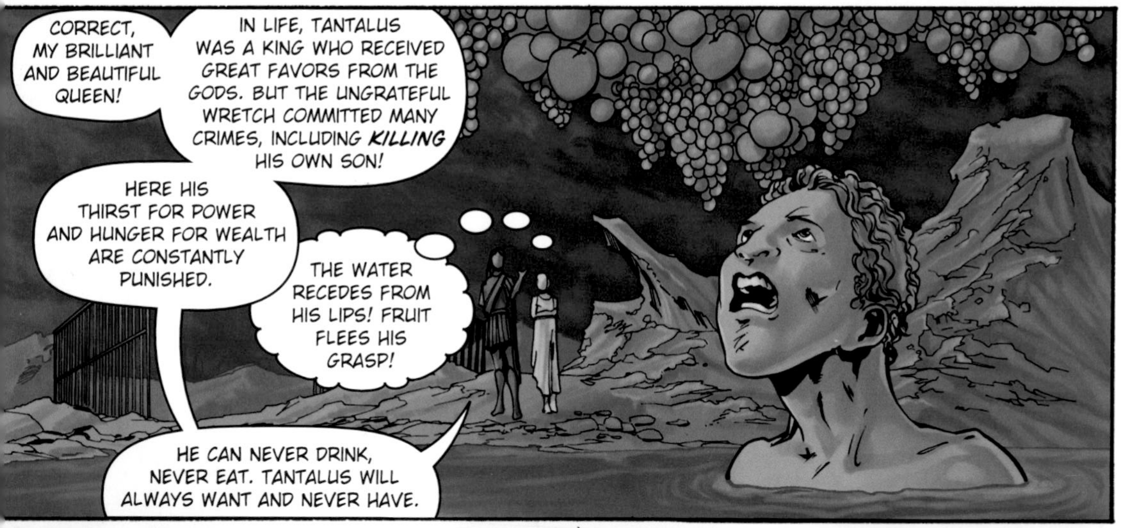
CORRECT, MY BRILLIANT AND BEAUTIFUL QUEEN!
IN LIFE, TANTALUS WAS A KING WHO RECEIVED GREAT FAVORS FROM THE GODS. BUT THE UNGRATEFUL WRETCH COMMITTED MANY CRIMES, INCLUDING *KILLING* HIS OWN SON!
HERE HIS THIRST FOR POWER AND HUNGER FOR WEALTH ARE CONSTANTLY PUNISHED.
THE WATER RECEDES FROM HIS LIPS! FRUIT FLEES HIS GRASP!
HE CAN NEVER DRINK, NEVER EAT. TANTALUS WILL ALWAYS WANT AND NEVER HAVE.

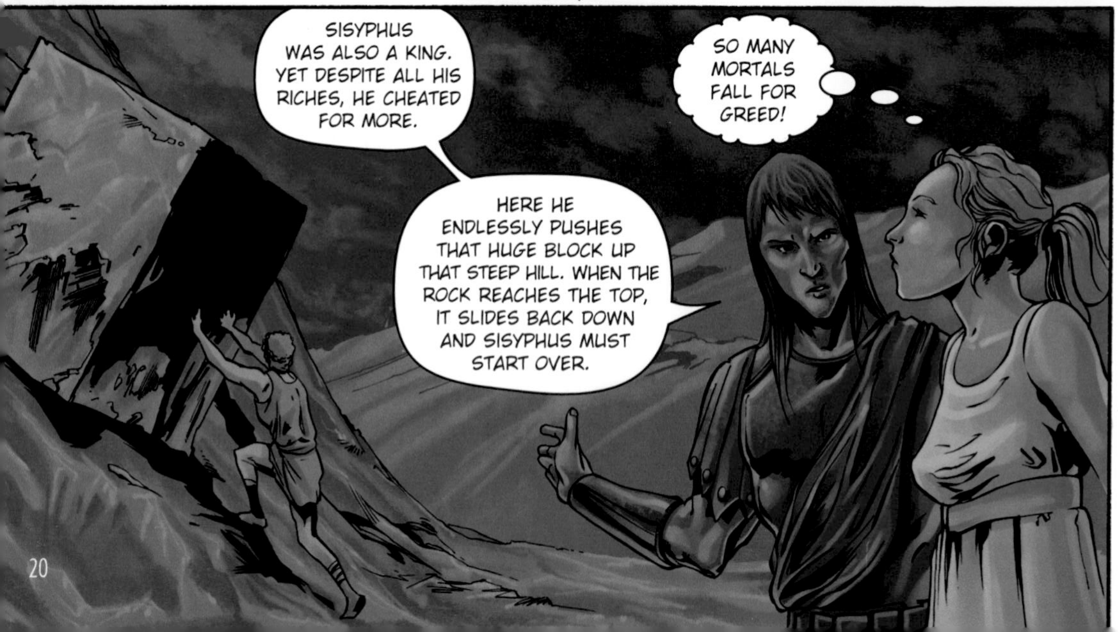
SISYPHUS WAS ALSO A KING. YET DESPITE ALL HIS RICHES, HE CHEATED FOR MORE.
SO MANY MORTALS FALL FOR GREED!
HERE HE ENDLESSLY PUSHES THAT HUGE BLOCK UP THAT STEEP HILL. WHEN THE ROCK REACHES THE TOP, IT SLIDES BACK DOWN AND SISYPHUS MUST START OVER.

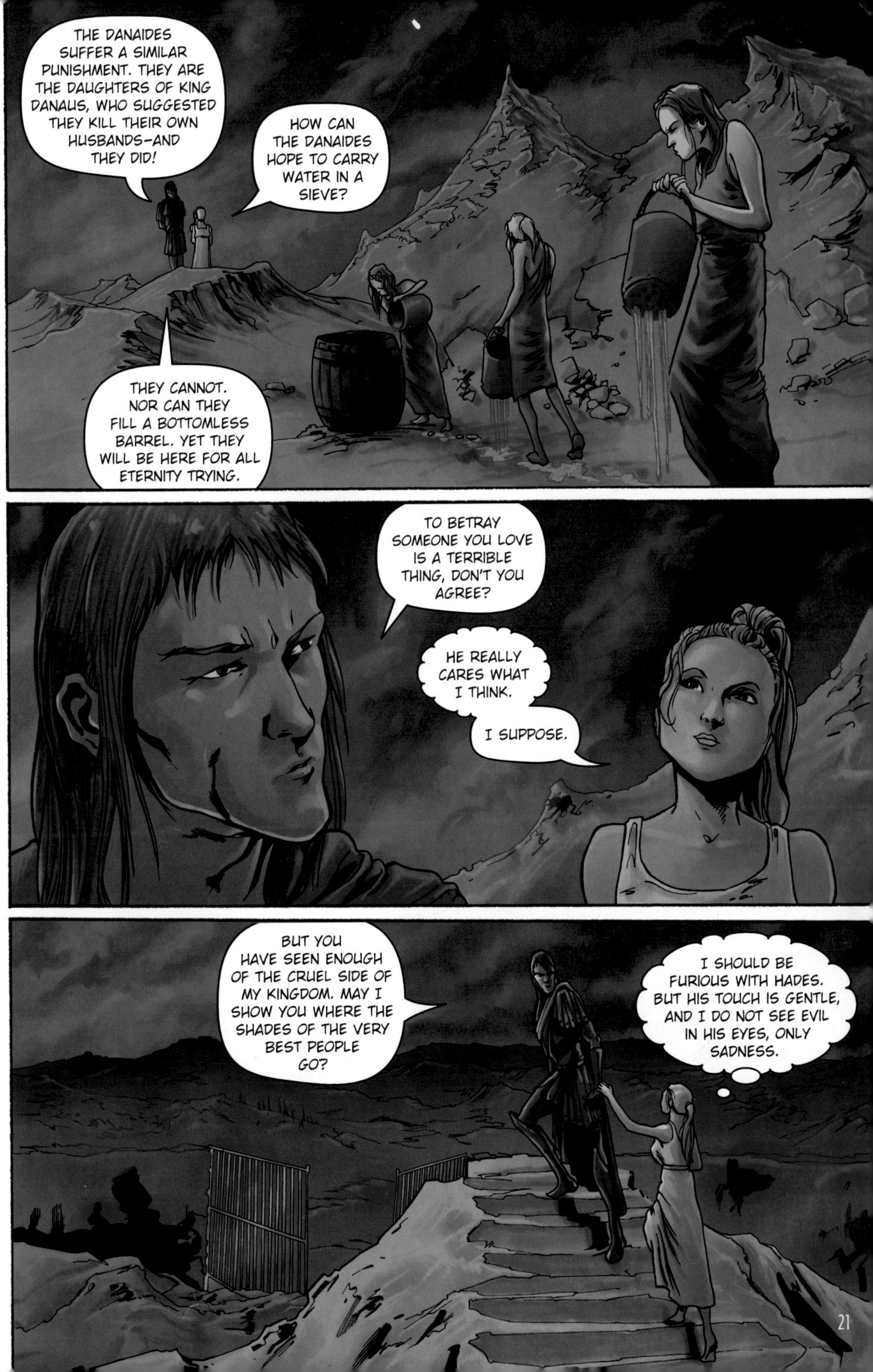
THE DANAIDES SUFFER A SIMILAR PUNISHMENT. THEY ARE THE DAUGHTERS OF KING DANAUS, WHO SUGGESTED THEY KILL THEIR OWN HUSBANDS—AND THEY DID!
HOW CAN THE DANAIDES HOPE TO CARRY WATER IN A SIEVE?
THEY CANNOT. NOR CAN THEY FILL A BOTTOMLESS BARREL. YET THEY WILL BE HERE FOR ALL ETERNITY TRYING.
TO BETRAY SOMEONE YOU LOVE IS A TERRIBLE THING, DON'T YOU AGREE?
HE REALLY CARES WHAT I THINK.
I SUPPOSE.
BUT YOU HAVE SEEN ENOUGH OF THE CRUEL SIDE OF MY KINGDOM. MAY I SHOW YOU WHERE THE SHADES OF THE VERY BEST PEOPLE GO?
I SHOULD BE FURIOUS WITH HADES. BUT HIS TOUCH IS GENTLE, AND I DO NOT SEE EVIL IN HIS EYES, ONLY SADNESS.

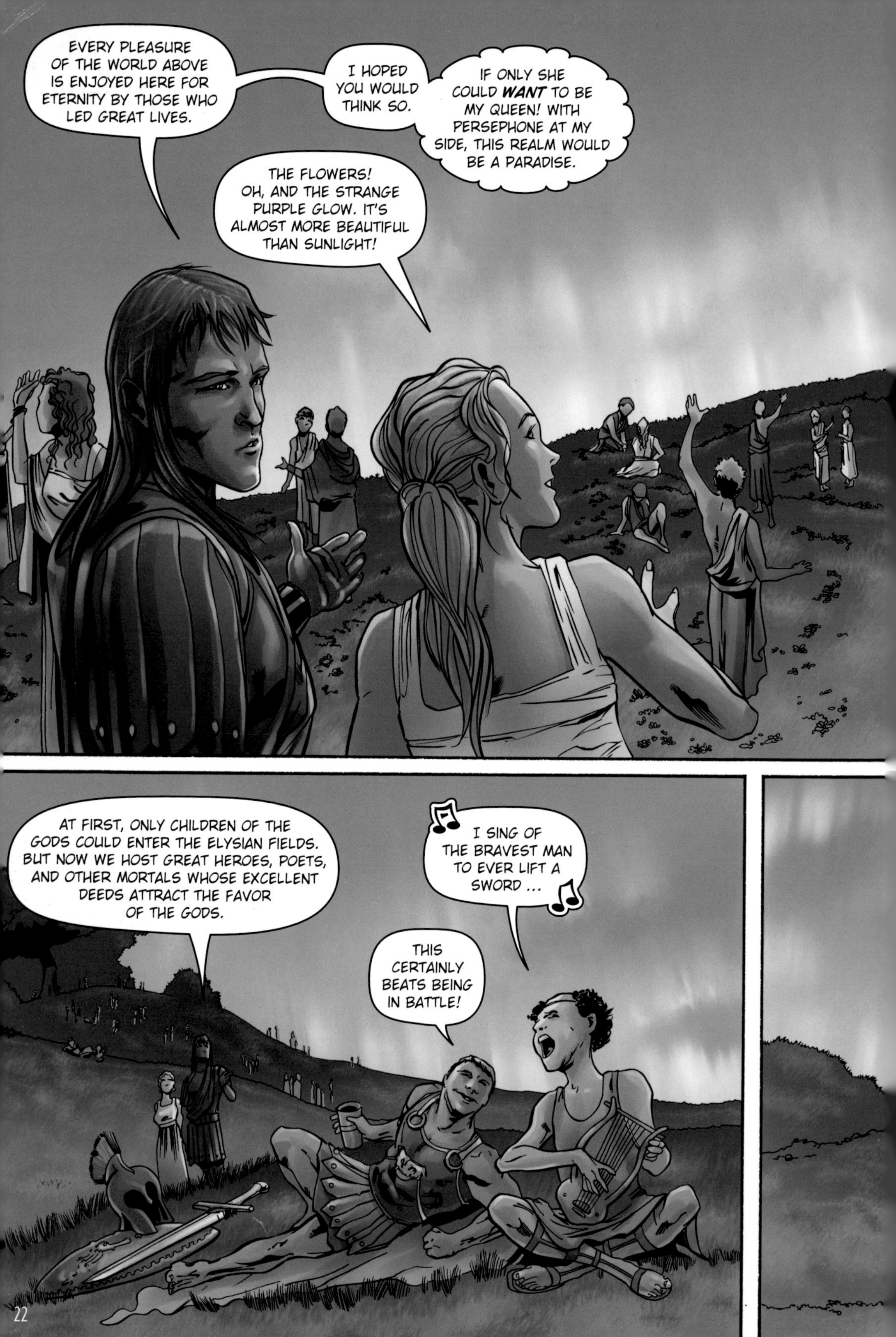
EVERY PLEASURE OF THE WORLD ABOVE IS ENJOYED HERE FOR ETERNITY BY THOSE WHO LED GREAT LIVES.
I HOPED YOU WOULD THINK SO.
IF ONLY SHE COULD **WANT** TO BE MY QUEEN! WITH PERSEPHONE AT MY SIDE, THIS REALM WOULD BE A PARADISE.
THE FLOWERS! OH, AND THE STRANGE PURPLE GLOW. IT'S ALMOST MORE BEAUTIFUL THAN SUNLIGHT!
AT FIRST, ONLY CHILDREN OF THE GODS COULD ENTER THE ELYSIAN FIELDS. BUT NOW WE HOST GREAT HEROES, POETS, AND OTHER MORTALS WHOSE EXCELLENT DEEDS ATTRACT THE FAVOR OF THE GODS.
I SING OF THE BRAVEST MAN TO EVER LIFT A SWORD ...
THIS CERTAINLY BEATS BEING IN BATTLE!

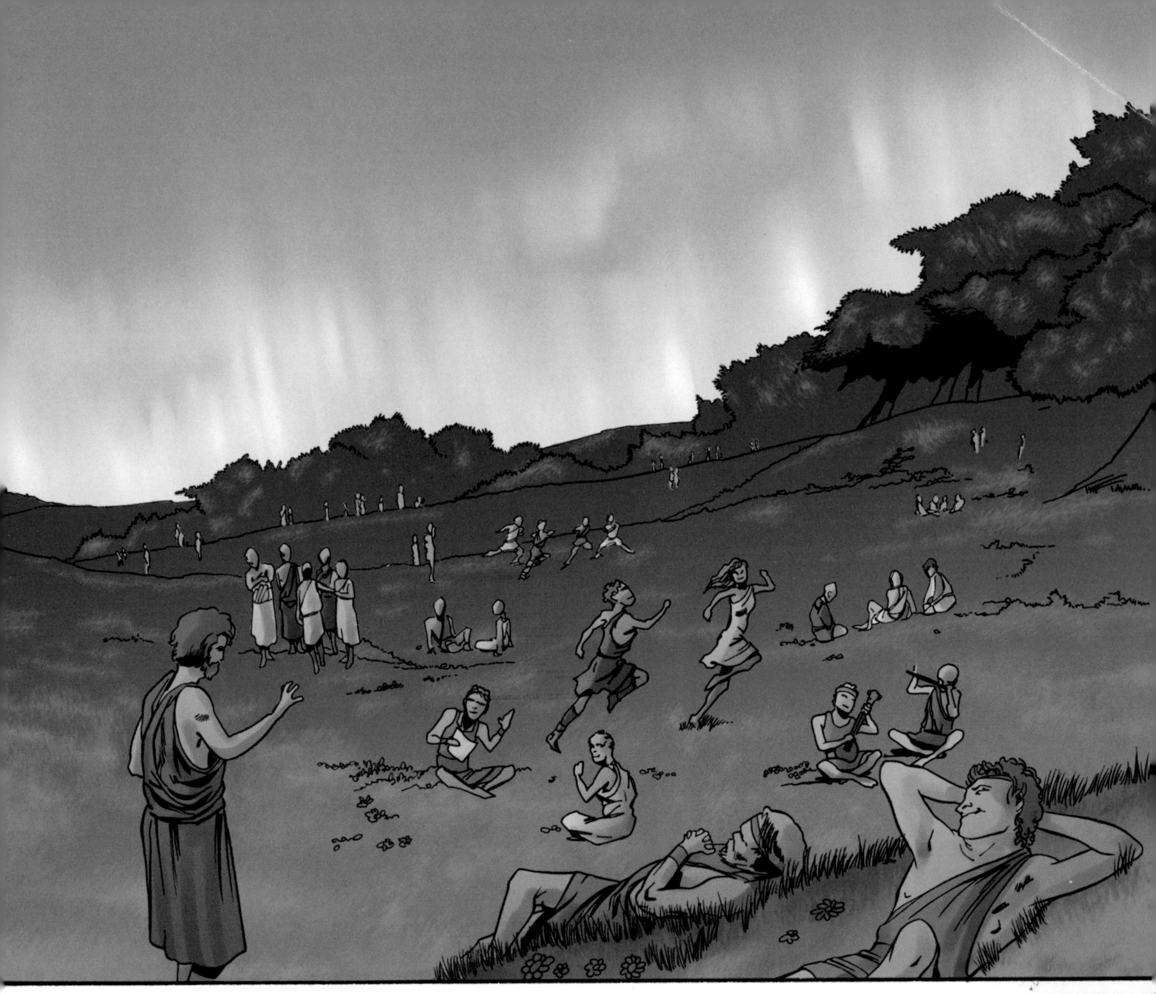

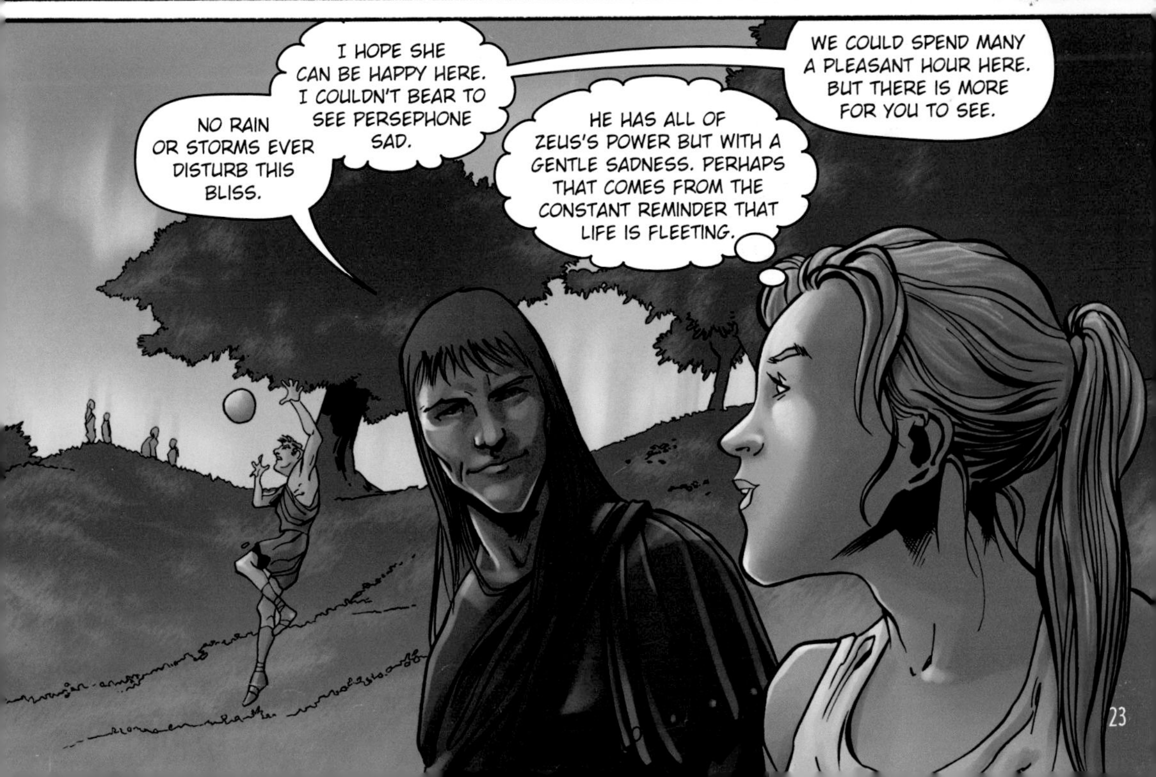
NO RAIN
OR STORMS EVER
DISTURB THIS
BLISS.
I HOPE SHE
CAN BE HAPPY HERE.
I COULDN'T BEAR TO
SEE PERSEPHONE
SAD.
HE HAS ALL OF
ZEUS'S POWER BUT WITH A
GENTLE SADNESS. PERHAPS
THAT COMES FROM THE
CONSTANT REMINDER THAT
LIFE IS FLEETING.
WE COULD SPEND MANY
A PLEASANT HOUR HERE.
BUT THERE IS MORE
FOR YOU TO SEE.

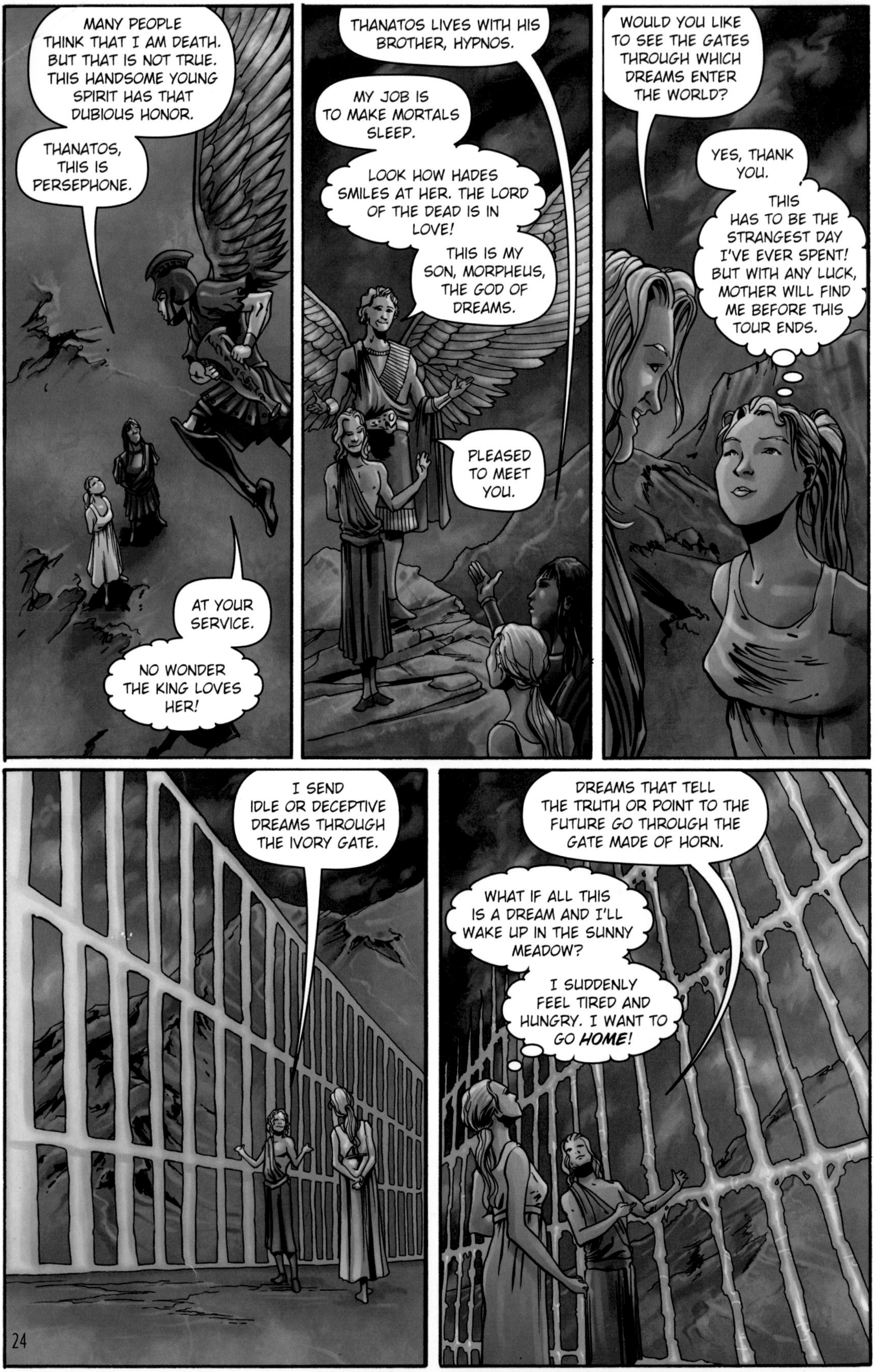
MANY PEOPLE THINK THAT I AM DEATH. BUT THAT IS NOT TRUE. THIS HANDSOME YOUNG SPIRIT HAS THAT DUBIOUS HONOR.
THANATOS, THIS IS PERSEPHONE.
AT YOUR SERVICE.
NO WONDER THE KING LOVES HER!
THANATOS LIVES WITH HIS BROTHER, HYPNOS.
MY JOB IS TO MAKE MORTALS SLEEP.
LOOK HOW HADES SMILES AT HER. THE LORD OF THE DEAD IS IN LOVE!
THIS IS MY SON, MORPHEUS, THE GOD OF DREAMS.
PLEASED TO MEET YOU.
WOULD YOU LIKE TO SEE THE GATES THROUGH WHICH DREAMS ENTER THE WORLD?
YES, THANK YOU.
THIS HAS TO BE THE STRANGEST DAY I'VE EVER SPENT! BUT WITH ANY LUCK, MOTHER WILL FIND ME BEFORE THIS TOUR ENDS.
I SEND IDLE OR DECEPTIVE DREAMS THROUGH THE IVORY GATE.
DREAMS THAT TELL THE TRUTH OR POINT TO THE FUTURE GO THROUGH THE GATE MADE OF HORN.
WHAT IF ALL THIS IS A DREAM AND I'LL WAKE UP IN THE SUNNY MEADOW?
I SUDDENLY FEEL TIRED AND HUNGRY. I WANT TO GO ***HOME***!

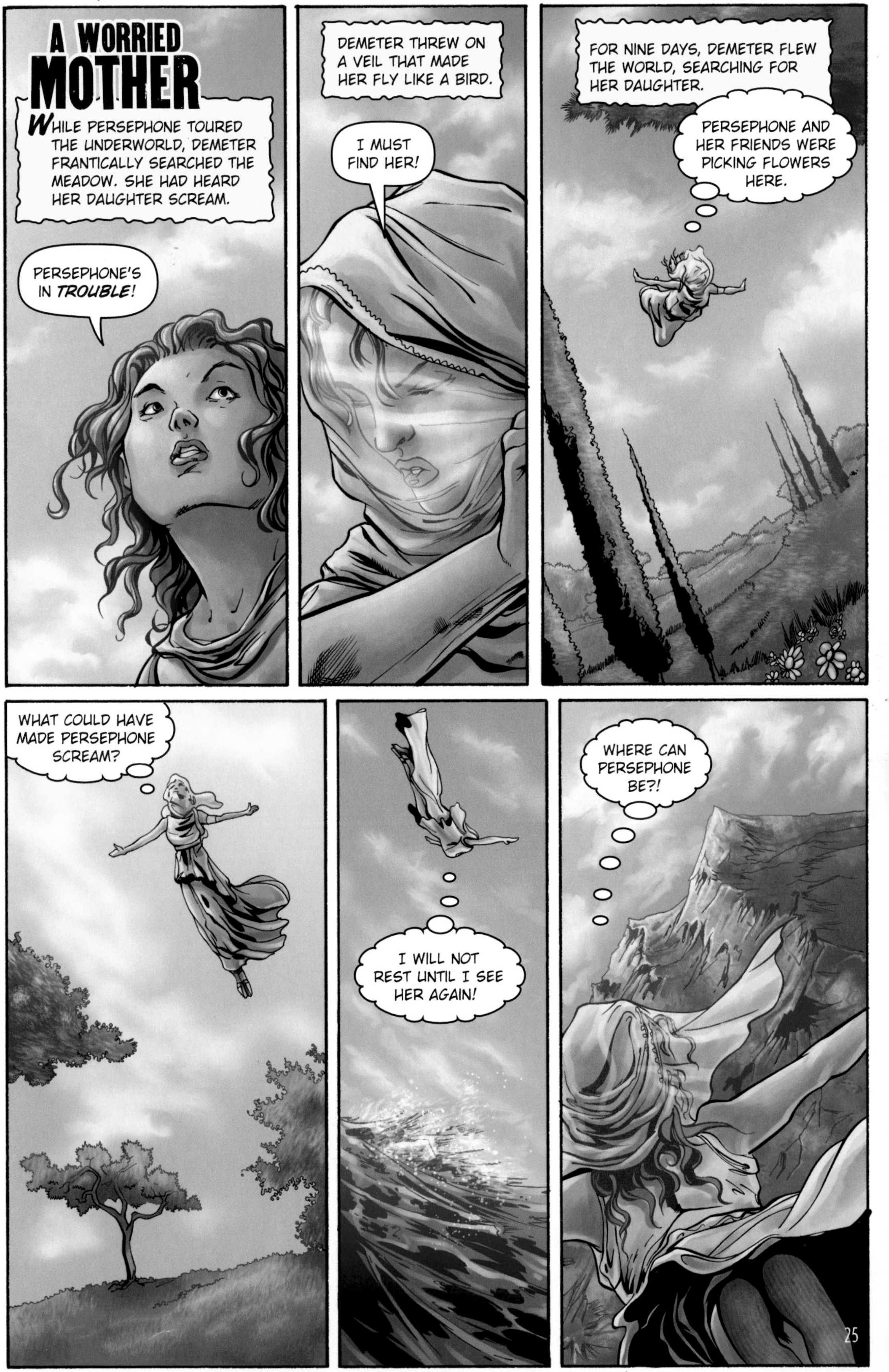
A WORRIED MOTHER
WHILE PERSEPHONE TOURED THE UNDERWORLD, DEMETER FRANTICALLY SEARCHED THE MEADOW. SHE HAD HEARD HER DAUGHTER SCREAM.
PERSEPHONE'S IN TROUBLE!
DEMETER THREW ON A VEIL THAT MADE HER FLY LIKE A BIRD.
I MUST FIND HER!
FOR NINE DAYS, DEMETER FLEW THE WORLD, SEARCHING FOR HER DAUGHTER.
PERSEPHONE AND HER FRIENDS WERE PICKING FLOWERS HERE.
WHAT COULD HAVE MADE PERSEPHONE SCREAM?
I WILL NOT REST UNTIL I SEE HER AGAIN!
WHERE CAN PERSEPHONE BE?!

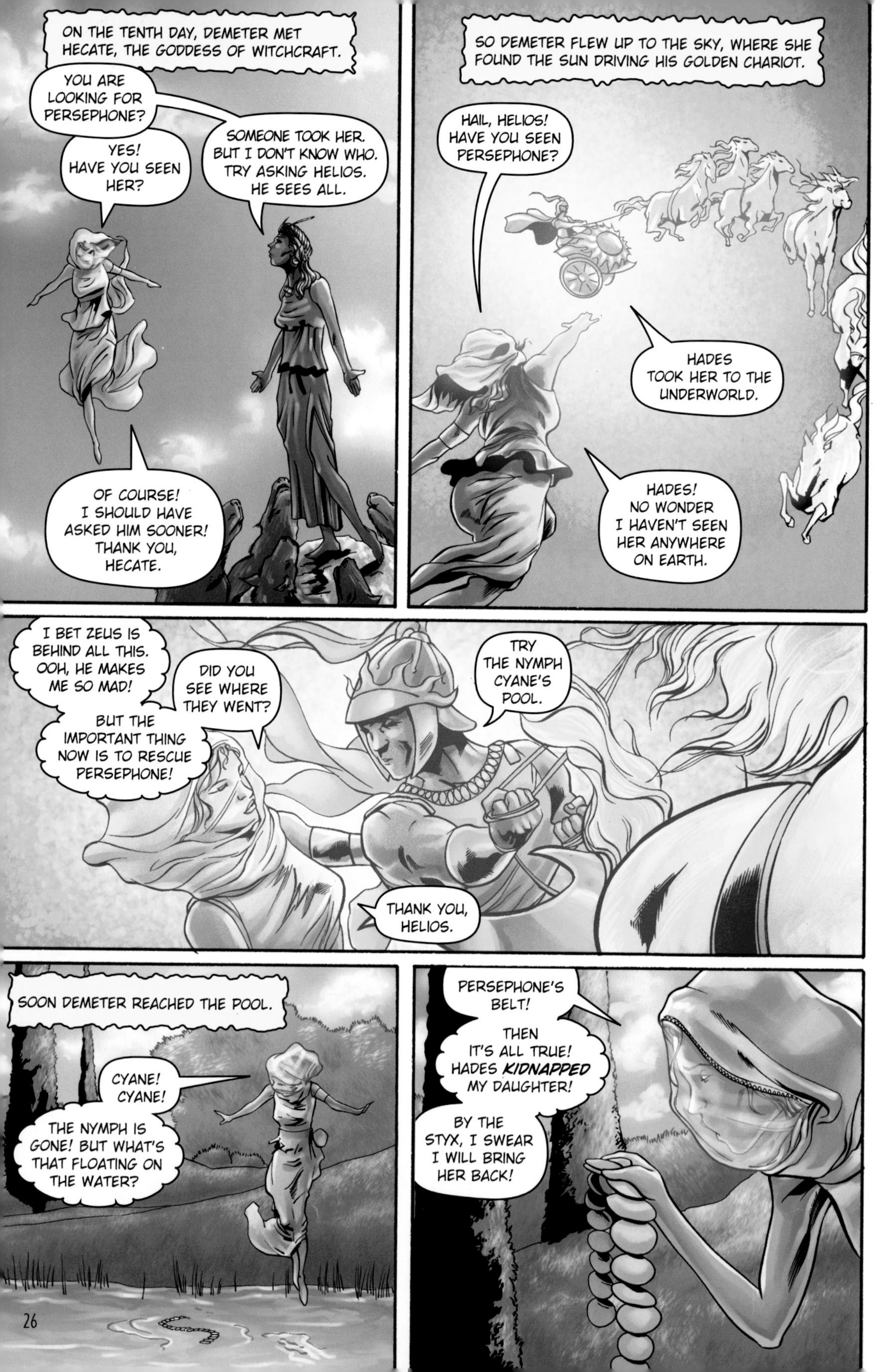
ON THE TENTH DAY, DEMETER MET HECATE, THE GODDESS OF WITCHCRAFT.
YOU ARE LOOKING FOR PERSEPHONE?
YES! HAVE YOU SEEN HER?
SOMEONE TOOK HER. BUT I DON'T KNOW WHO. TRY ASKING HELIOS. HE SEES ALL.
OF COURSE! I SHOULD HAVE ASKED HIM SOONER! THANK YOU, HECATE.
SO DEMETER FLEW UP TO THE SKY, WHERE SHE FOUND THE SUN DRIVING HIS GOLDEN CHARIOT.
HAIL, HELIOS! HAVE YOU SEEN PERSEPHONE?
HADES TOOK HER TO THE UNDERWORLD.
HADES! NO WONDER I HAVEN'T SEEN HER ANYWHERE ON EARTH.
I BET ZEUS IS BEHIND ALL THIS. OOH, HE MAKES ME SO MAD!
BUT THE IMPORTANT THING NOW IS TO RESCUE PERSEPHONE!
DID YOU SEE WHERE THEY WENT?
TRY THE NYMPH CYANE'S POOL.
THANK YOU, HELIOS.
SOON DEMETER REACHED THE POOL.
CYANE! CYANE!
THE NYMPH IS GONE! BUT WHAT'S THAT FLOATING ON THE WATER?
PERSEPHONE'S BELT!
THEN IT'S ALL TRUE! HADES ***KIDNAPPED*** MY DAUGHTER!
BY THE STYX, I SWEAR I WILL BRING HER BACK!

DEMETER WENT STRAIGHT TO ZEUS.

YOU MUST MAKE HADES *RETURN* PERSEPHONE! HOW COULD YOU GIVE AWAY MY ONLY CHILD?

I WAS JUST TRYING TO MAKE MY BROTHER HAPPY.

THERE'S NOTHING I CAN DO. YOU MUST UNDERSTAND.

ARE YOU SAYING THE KING OF THE GODS IS *HELPLESS*?

THIS IS WHAT MY HUSBAND'S UNFAITHFULNESS BRINGS—MOTHERS AND CHILDREN ALWAYS TURNING UP FOR FAVORS.

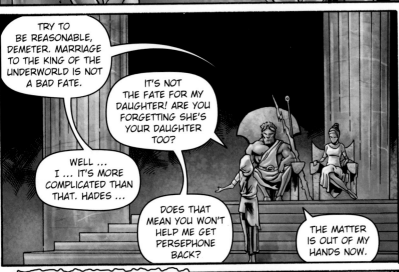

TRY TO BE REASONABLE, DEMETER. MARRIAGE TO THE KING OF THE UNDERWORLD IS NOT A BAD FATE.

IT'S NOT THE FATE FOR MY DAUGHTER! ARE YOU FORGETTING SHE'S YOUR DAUGHTER TOO?

WELL ... I ... IT'S MORE COMPLICATED THAN THAT. HADES ...

DOES THAT MEAN YOU WON'T HELP ME GET PERSEPHONE BACK?

THE MATTER IS OUT OF MY HANDS NOW.

I WON'T STAY ON MOUNT OLYMPUS ANOTHER *MINUTE*! I WOULD RATHER BE AMONG THE FOOLISH MORTALS THAN THE PITILESS GODS.

SOMETIMES THE GODS DISGUISED THEMSELVES AS MORTALS.

THE MORTALS MAY SOMEHOW HELP ME RESCUE PERSEPHONE—OR AT LEAST DISTRACT ME FROM MY GRIEF UNTIL I CAN FORM A PLAN.

GODS AND GODDESSES DRANK NECTAR AND LIVED ON A FOOD CALLED AMBROSIA.

THIS HEAT AND DUST! I FEEL LIKE I'M WILTING. SMALL WONDER, I HAVEN'T TASTED AMBROSIA OR NECTAR SINCE PERSEPHONE DISAPPEARED.

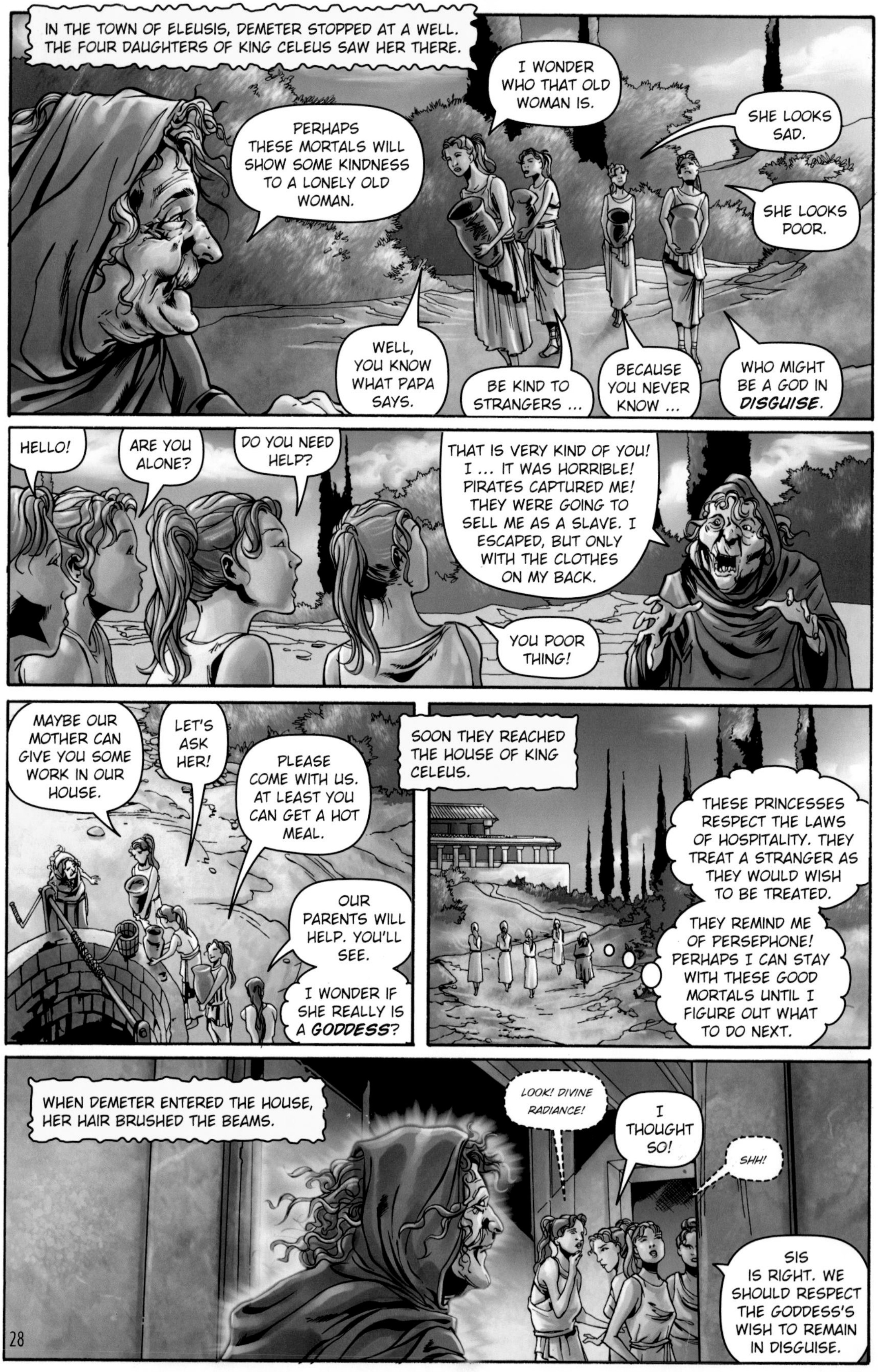
IN THE TOWN OF ELEUSIS, DEMETER STOPPED AT A WELL. THE FOUR DAUGHTERS OF KING CELEUS SAW HER THERE.
PERHAPS THESE MORTALS WILL SHOW SOME KINDNESS TO A LONELY OLD WOMAN.
I WONDER WHO THAT OLD WOMAN IS.
SHE LOOKS SAD.
SHE LOOKS POOR.
WELL, YOU KNOW WHAT PAPA SAYS.
BE KIND TO STRANGERS ...
BECAUSE YOU NEVER KNOW ...
WHO MIGHT BE A GOD IN *DISGUISE*.
HELLO!
ARE YOU ALONE?
DO YOU NEED HELP?
THAT IS VERY KIND OF YOU! I ... IT WAS HORRIBLE! PIRATES CAPTURED ME! THEY WERE GOING TO SELL ME AS A SLAVE. I ESCAPED, BUT ONLY WITH THE CLOTHES ON MY BACK.
YOU POOR THING!
MAYBE OUR MOTHER CAN GIVE YOU SOME WORK IN OUR HOUSE.
LET'S ASK HER!
PLEASE COME WITH US. AT LEAST YOU CAN GET A HOT MEAL.
OUR PARENTS WILL HELP. YOU'LL SEE.
I WONDER IF SHE REALLY IS A *GODDESS*?
SOON THEY REACHED THE HOUSE OF KING CELEUS.
THESE PRINCESSES RESPECT THE LAWS OF HOSPITALITY. THEY TREAT A STRANGER AS THEY WOULD WISH TO BE TREATED.
THEY REMIND ME OF PERSEPHONE! PERHAPS I CAN STAY WITH THESE GOOD MORTALS UNTIL I FIGURE OUT WHAT TO DO NEXT.
WHEN DEMETER ENTERED THE HOUSE, HER HAIR BRUSHED THE BEAMS.
LOOK! DIVINE RADIANCE!
I THOUGHT SO!
SHH!
SIS IS RIGHT. WE SHOULD RESPECT THE GODDESS'S WISH TO REMAIN IN DISGUISE.

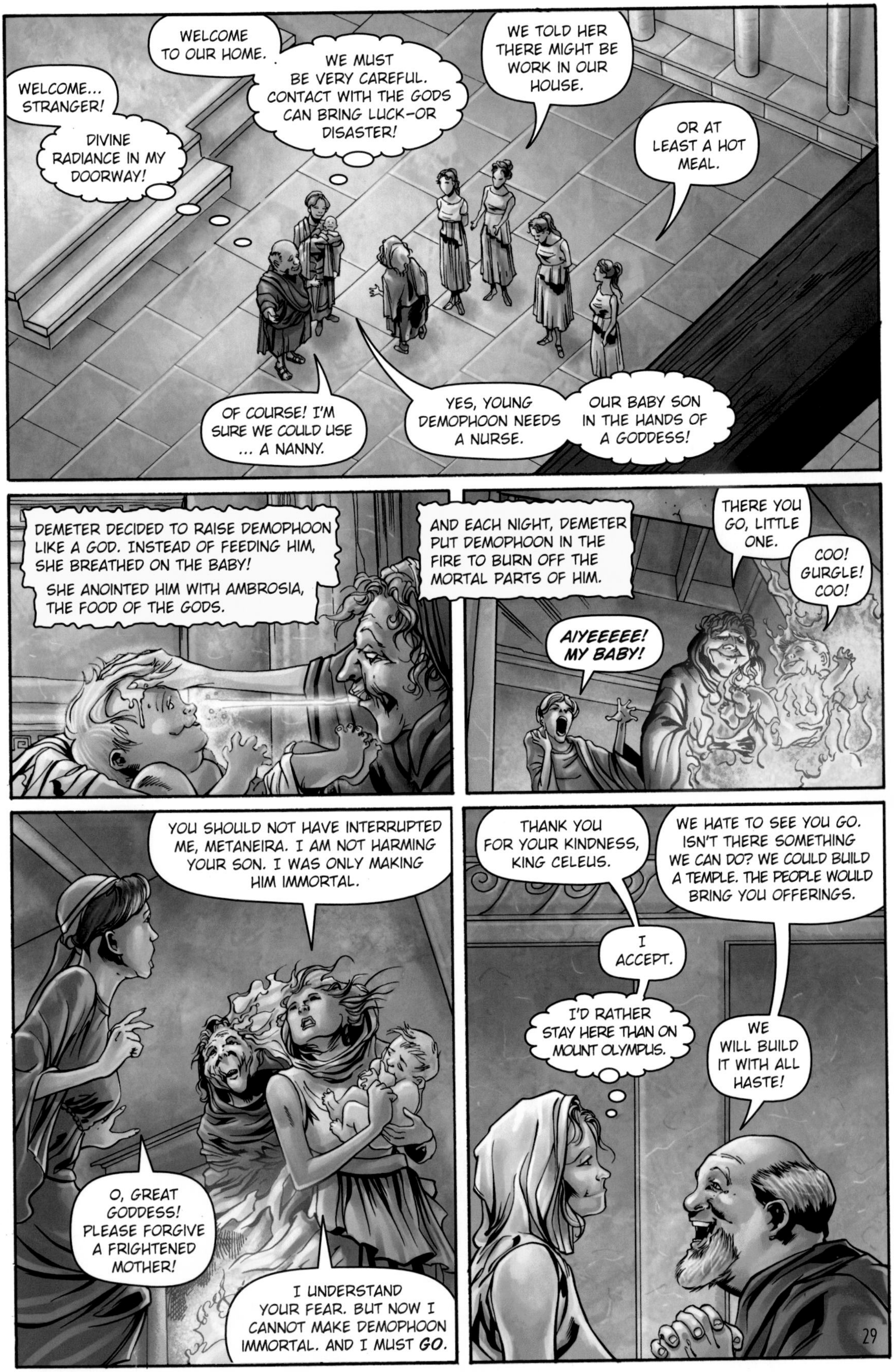
WELCOME... STRANGER!
DIVINE RADIANCE IN MY DOORWAY!
WELCOME TO OUR HOME.
WE MUST BE VERY CAREFUL. CONTACT WITH THE GODS CAN BRING LUCK—OR DISASTER!
WE TOLD HER THERE MIGHT BE WORK IN OUR HOUSE.
OR AT LEAST A HOT MEAL.
OF COURSE! I'M SURE WE COULD USE ... A NANNY.
YES, YOUNG DEMOPHOON NEEDS A NURSE.
OUR BABY SON IN THE HANDS OF A GODDESS!
DEMETER DECIDED TO RAISE DEMOPHOON LIKE A GOD. INSTEAD OF FEEDING HIM, SHE BREATHED ON THE BABY!
SHE ANOINTED HIM WITH AMBROSIA, THE FOOD OF THE GODS.
AND EACH NIGHT, DEMETER PUT DEMOPHOON IN THE FIRE TO BURN OFF THE MORTAL PARTS OF HIM.
THERE YOU GO, LITTLE ONE.
COO! GURGLE! COO!
AIYEEEEE! MY BABY!
YOU SHOULD NOT HAVE INTERRUPTED ME, METANEIRA. I AM NOT HARMING YOUR SON. I WAS ONLY MAKING HIM IMMORTAL.
O, GREAT GODDESS! PLEASE FORGIVE A FRIGHTENED MOTHER!
I UNDERSTAND YOUR FEAR. BUT NOW I CANNOT MAKE DEMOPHOON IMMORTAL. AND I MUST GO.
THANK YOU FOR YOUR KINDNESS, KING CELEUS.
WE HATE TO SEE YOU GO. ISN'T THERE SOMETHING WE CAN DO? WE COULD BUILD A TEMPLE. THE PEOPLE WOULD BRING YOU OFFERINGS.
I ACCEPT.
I'D RATHER STAY HERE THAN ON MOUNT OLYMPUS.
WE WILL BUILD IT WITH ALL HASTE!

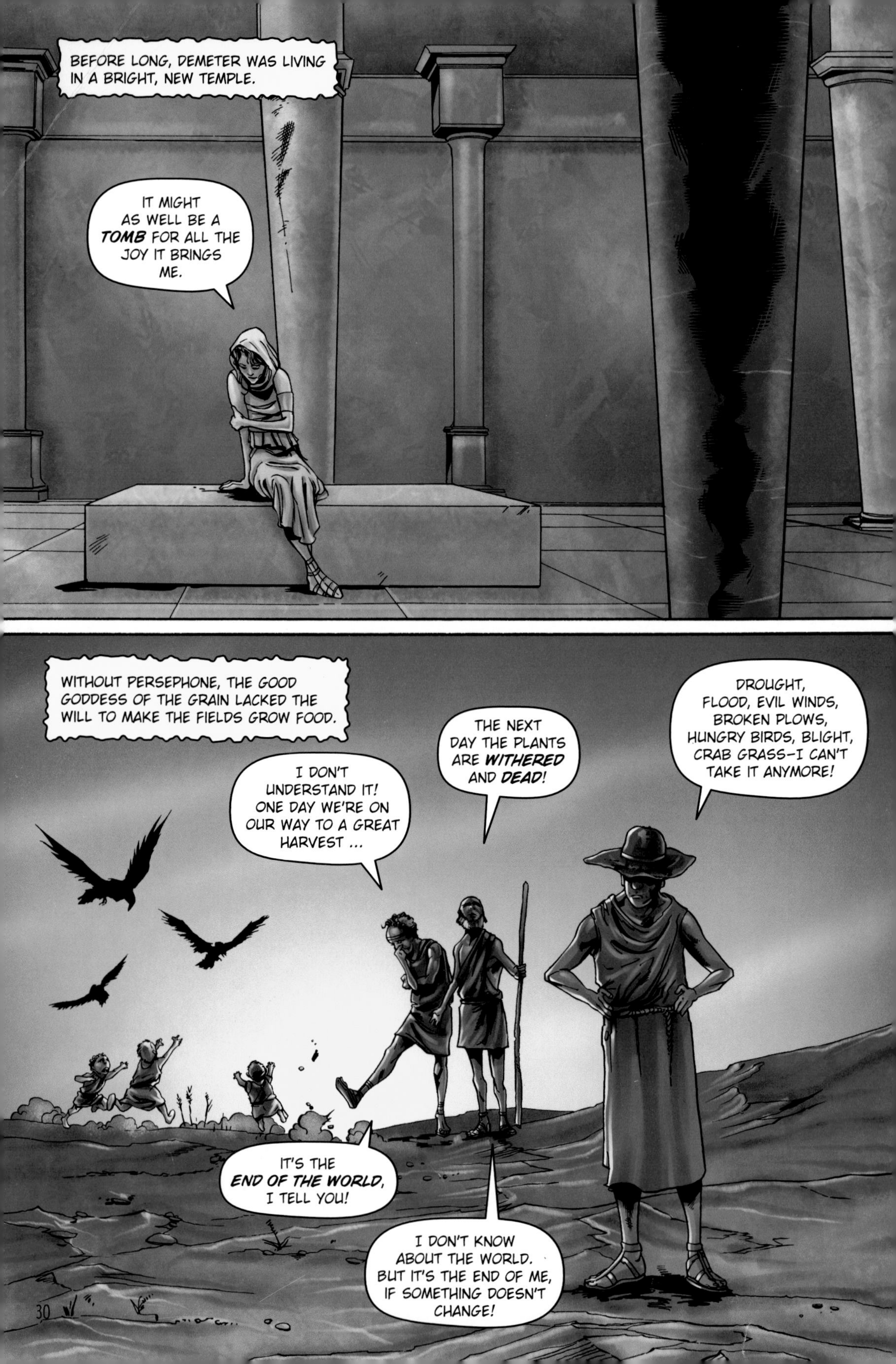
BEFORE LONG, DEMETER WAS LIVING IN A BRIGHT, NEW TEMPLE.
IT MIGHT AS WELL BE A *TOMB* FOR ALL THE JOY IT BRINGS ME.
WITHOUT PERSEPHONE, THE GOOD GODDESS OF THE GRAIN LACKED THE WILL TO MAKE THE FIELDS GROW FOOD.
I DON'T UNDERSTAND IT! ONE DAY WE'RE ON OUR WAY TO A GREAT HARVEST ...
THE NEXT DAY THE PLANTS ARE *WITHERED* AND *DEAD*!
DROUGHT, FLOOD, EVIL WINDS, BROKEN PLOWS, HUNGRY BIRDS, BLIGHT, CRAB GRASS—I CAN'T TAKE IT ANYMORE!
IT'S THE *END OF THE WORLD*, I TELL YOU!
I DON'T KNOW ABOUT THE WORLD. BUT IT'S THE END OF ME, IF SOMETHING DOESN'T CHANGE!

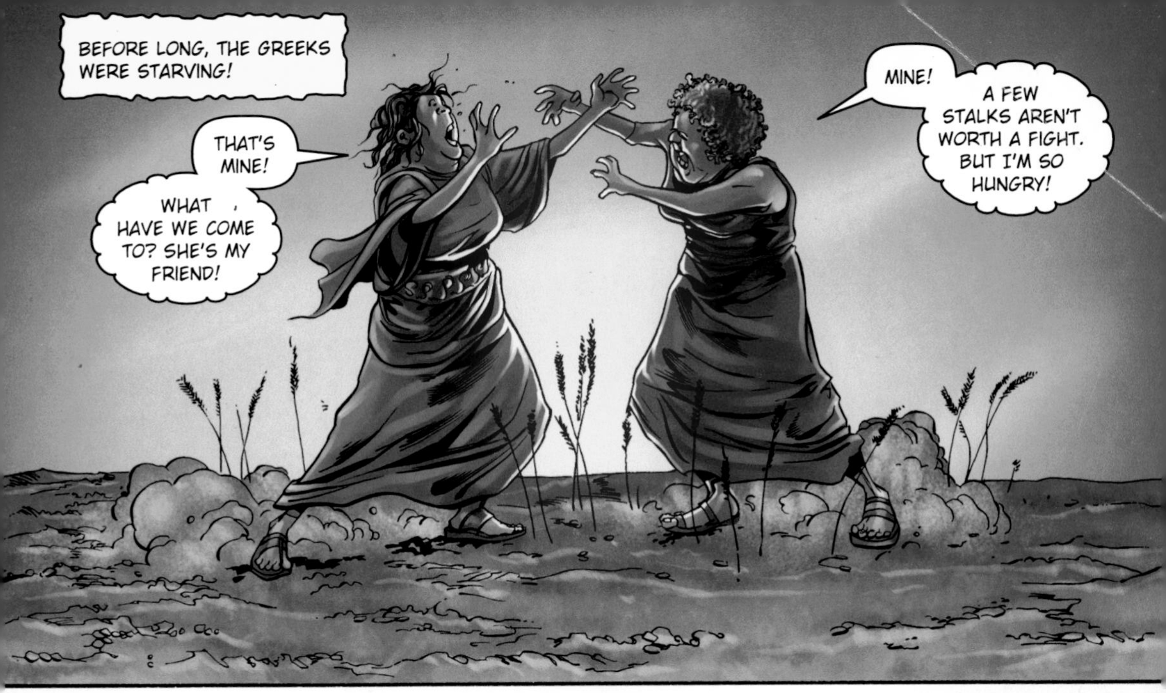
BEFORE LONG, THE GREEKS WERE STARVING!
THAT'S MINE!
WHAT HAVE WE COME TO? SHE'S MY FRIEND!
MINE!
A FEW STALKS AREN'T WORTH A FIGHT. BUT I'M SO HUNGRY!

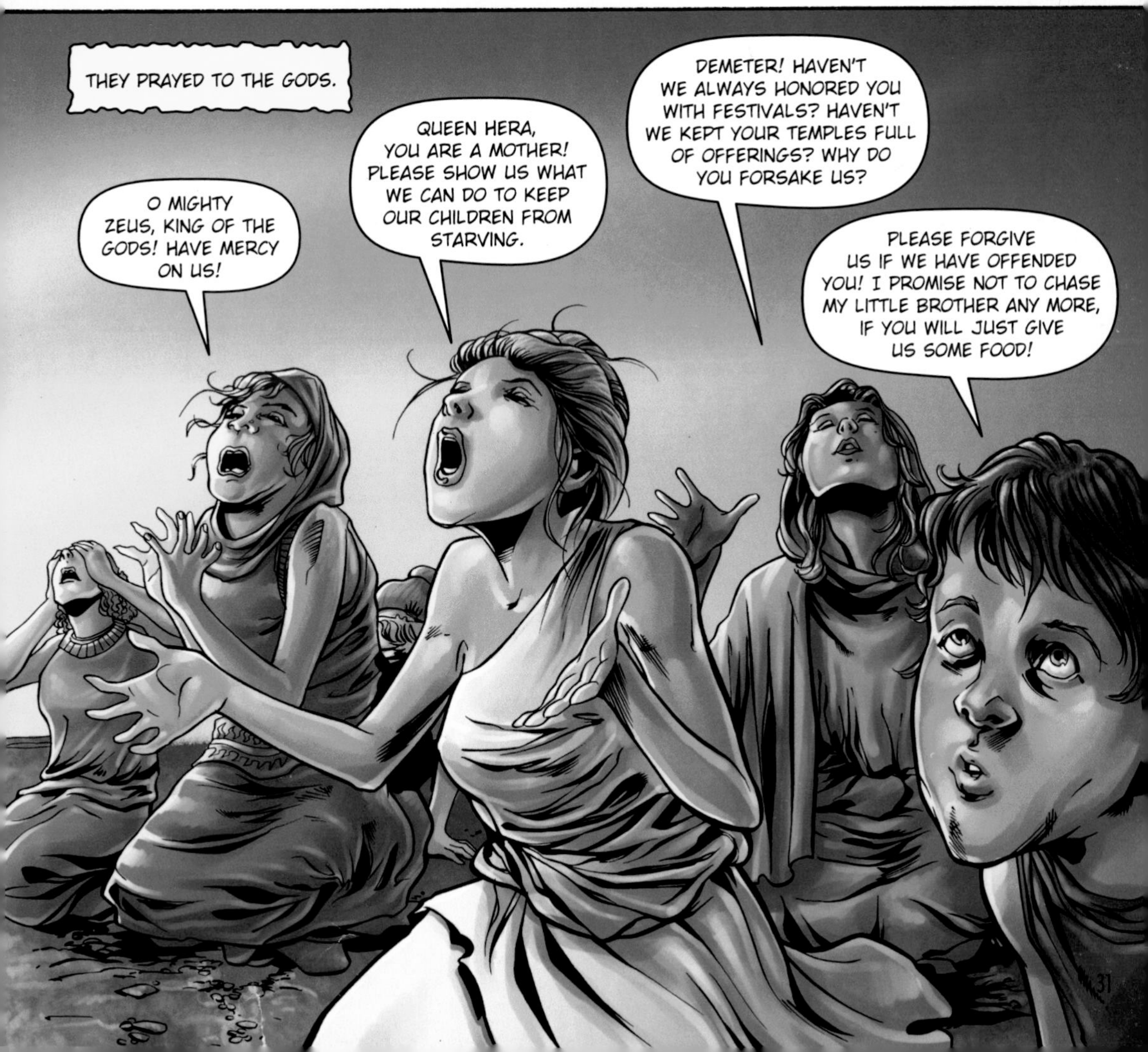
THEY PRAYED TO THE GODS.
O MIGHTY ZEUS, KING OF THE GODS! HAVE MERCY ON US!
QUEEN HERA, YOU ARE A MOTHER! PLEASE SHOW US WHAT WE CAN DO TO KEEP OUR CHILDREN FROM STARVING.
DEMETER! HAVEN'T WE ALWAYS HONORED YOU WITH FESTIVALS? HAVEN'T WE KEPT YOUR TEMPLES FULL OF OFFERINGS? WHY DO YOU FORSAKE US?
PLEASE FORGIVE US IF WE HAVE OFFENDED YOU! I PROMISE NOT TO CHASE MY LITTLE BROTHER ANY MORE, IF YOU WILL JUST GIVE US SOME FOOD!

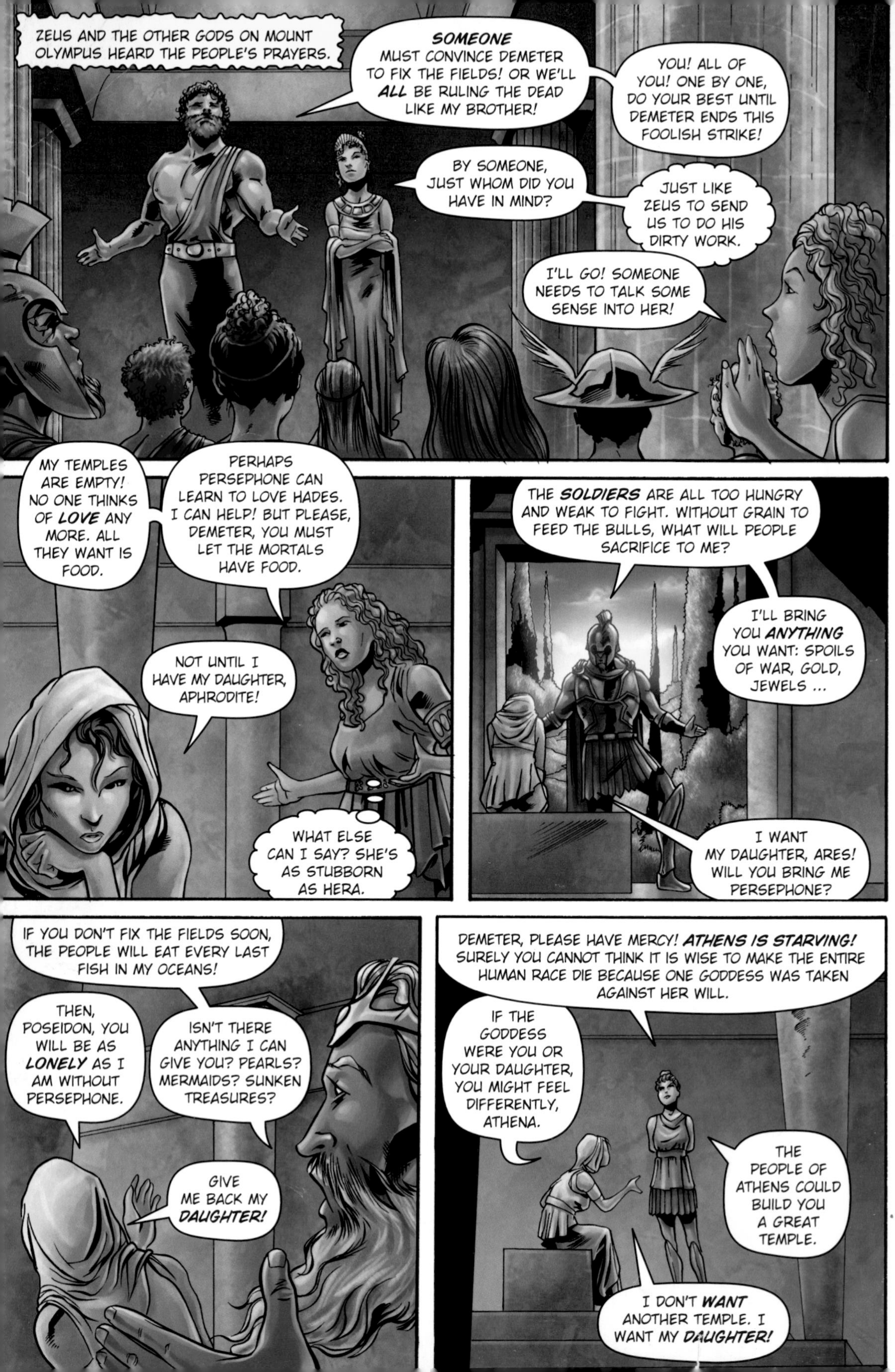
ZEUS AND THE OTHER GODS ON MOUNT OLYMPUS HEARD THE PEOPLE'S PRAYERS.
SOMEONE MUST CONVINCE DEMETER TO FIX THE FIELDS! OR WE'LL ALL BE RULING THE DEAD LIKE MY BROTHER!
YOU! ALL OF YOU! ONE BY ONE, DO YOUR BEST UNTIL DEMETER ENDS THIS FOOLISH STRIKE!
BY SOMEONE, JUST WHOM DID YOU HAVE IN MIND?
JUST LIKE ZEUS TO SEND US TO DO HIS DIRTY WORK.
I'LL GO! SOMEONE NEEDS TO TALK SOME SENSE INTO HER!
MY TEMPLES ARE EMPTY! NO ONE THINKS OF LOVE ANY MORE. ALL THEY WANT IS FOOD.
PERHAPS PERSEPHONE CAN LEARN TO LOVE HADES. I CAN HELP! BUT PLEASE, DEMETER, YOU MUST LET THE MORTALS HAVE FOOD.
NOT UNTIL I HAVE MY DAUGHTER, APHRODITE!
WHAT ELSE CAN I SAY? SHE'S AS STUBBORN AS HERA.
THE SOLDIERS ARE ALL TOO HUNGRY AND WEAK TO FIGHT. WITHOUT GRAIN TO FEED THE BULLS, WHAT WILL PEOPLE SACRIFICE TO ME?
I'LL BRING YOU ANYTHING YOU WANT: SPOILS OF WAR, GOLD, JEWELS ...
I WANT MY DAUGHTER, ARES! WILL YOU BRING ME PERSEPHONE?
IF YOU DON'T FIX THE FIELDS SOON, THE PEOPLE WILL EAT EVERY LAST FISH IN MY OCEANS!
THEN, POSEIDON, YOU WILL BE AS LONELY AS I AM WITHOUT PERSEPHONE.
ISN'T THERE ANYTHING I CAN GIVE YOU? PEARLS? MERMAIDS? SUNKEN TREASURES?
GIVE ME BACK MY DAUGHTER!
DEMETER, PLEASE HAVE MERCY! ATHENS IS STARVING! SURELY YOU CANNOT THINK IT IS WISE TO MAKE THE ENTIRE HUMAN RACE DIE BECAUSE ONE GODDESS WAS TAKEN AGAINST HER WILL.
IF THE GODDESS WERE YOU OR YOUR DAUGHTER, YOU MIGHT FEEL DIFFERENTLY, ATHENA.
THE PEOPLE OF ATHENS COULD BUILD YOU A GREAT TEMPLE.
I DON'T WANT ANOTHER TEMPLE. I WANT MY DAUGHTER!

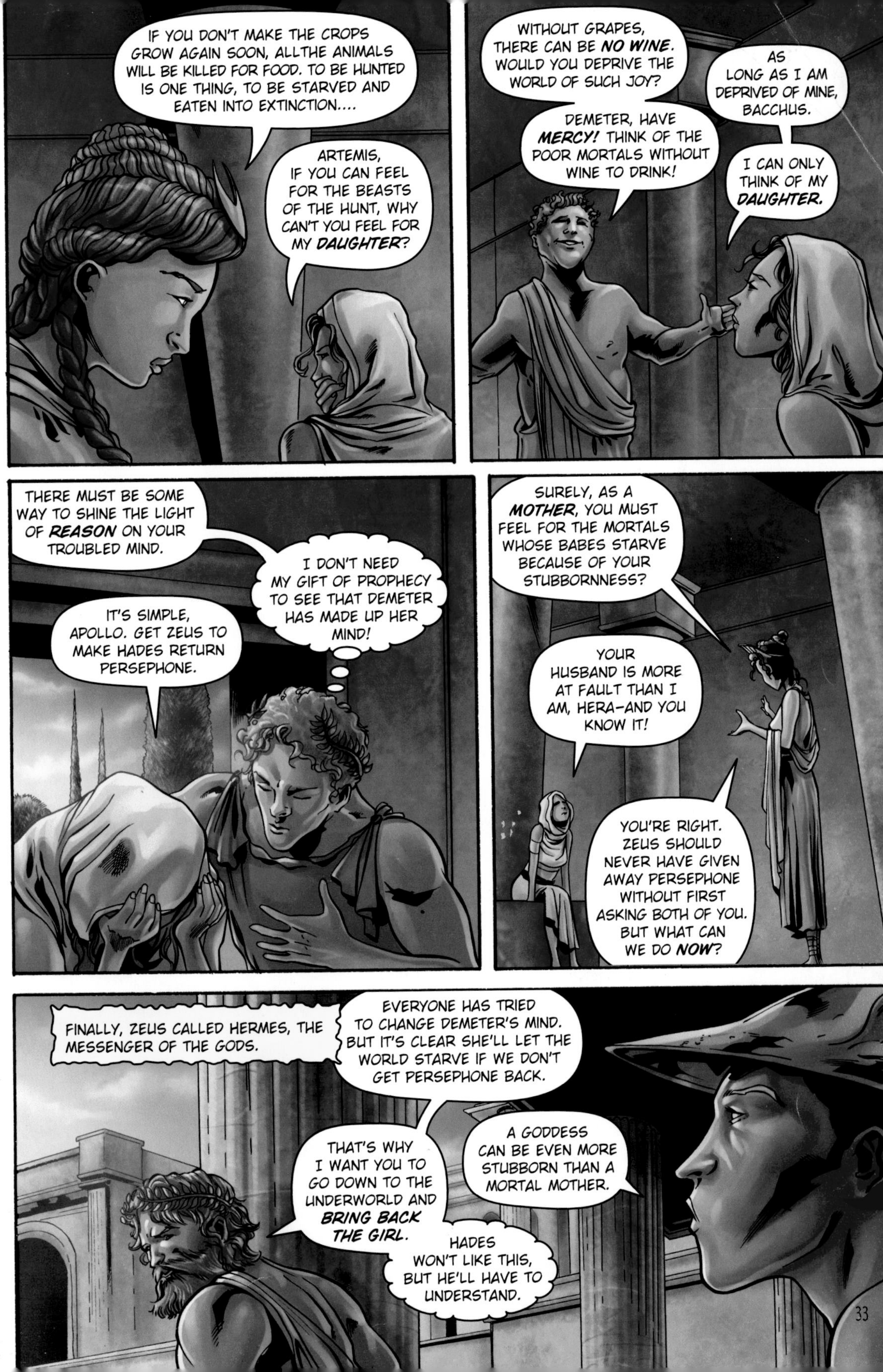
IF YOU DON'T MAKE THE CROPS GROW AGAIN SOON, ALLTHE ANIMALS WILL BE KILLED FOR FOOD. TO BE HUNTED IS ONE THING, TO BE STARVED AND EATEN INTO EXTINCTION....
ARTEMIS, IF YOU CAN FEEL FOR THE BEASTS OF THE HUNT, WHY CAN'T YOU FEEL FOR MY DAUGHTER?
WITHOUT GRAPES, THERE CAN BE NO WINE. WOULD YOU DEPRIVE THE WORLD OF SUCH JOY?
AS LONG AS I AM DEPRIVED OF MINE, BACCHUS.
DEMETER, HAVE MERCY! THINK OF THE POOR MORTALS WITHOUT WINE TO DRINK!
I CAN ONLY THINK OF MY DAUGHTER.
THERE MUST BE SOME WAY TO SHINE THE LIGHT OF REASON ON YOUR TROUBLED MIND.
I DON'T NEED MY GIFT OF PROPHECY TO SEE THAT DEMETER HAS MADE UP HER MIND!
IT'S SIMPLE, APOLLO. GET ZEUS TO MAKE HADES RETURN PERSEPHONE.
SURELY, AS A MOTHER, YOU MUST FEEL FOR THE MORTALS WHOSE BABES STARVE BECAUSE OF YOUR STUBBORNNESS?
YOUR HUSBAND IS MORE AT FAULT THAN I AM, HERA—AND YOU KNOW IT!
YOU'RE RIGHT. ZEUS SHOULD NEVER HAVE GIVEN AWAY PERSEPHONE WITHOUT FIRST ASKING BOTH OF YOU. BUT WHAT CAN WE DO NOW?
FINALLY, ZEUS CALLED HERMES, THE MESSENGER OF THE GODS.
EVERYONE HAS TRIED TO CHANGE DEMETER'S MIND. BUT IT'S CLEAR SHE'LL LET THE WORLD STARVE IF WE DON'T GET PERSEPHONE BACK.
A GODDESS CAN BE EVEN MORE STUBBORN THAN A MORTAL MOTHER.
THAT'S WHY I WANT YOU TO GO DOWN TO THE UNDERWORLD AND BRING BACK THE GIRL.
HADES WON'T LIKE THIS, BUT HE'LL HAVE TO UNDERSTAND.

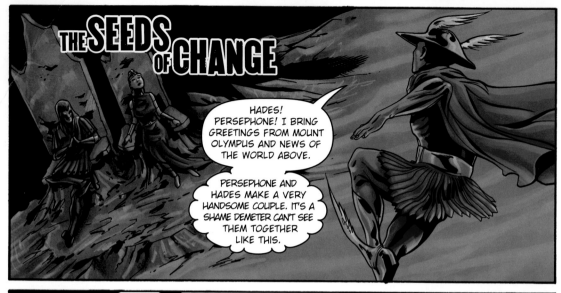

HADES! PERSEPHONE! I BRING GREETINGS FROM MOUNT OLYMPUS AND NEWS OF THE WORLD ABOVE.

PERSEPHONE AND HADES MAKE A VERY HANDSOME COUPLE. IT'S A SHAME DEMETER CAN'T SEE THEM TOGETHER LIKE THIS.

HERMES! HOW IS MY MOTHER?

DEMETER HAS FROZEN THE WORLD IN GRIEF AT YOUR ABSENCE. THE MORTALS ARE STARVING. EVERY GOD, INCLUDING YOUR FATHER, BEGS YOU TO RETURN AT ONCE.

HOW COULD *I* BE SO IMPORTANT TO THE GODS? BUT I GUESS MOTHER IS IMPORTANT.

PERSEPHONE IS MY QUEEN! ZEUS *PROMISED* HER TO ME.

BUT HE DID NOT ASK DEMETER OR PERSEPHONE. SO THE MARRIAGE CANNOT BE.

I'D ALMOST FORGOTTEN HOW FRIGHTENING IT WAS TO BE GRABBED AGAINST MY WILL. HADES HAS BEEN SO KIND.

BUT I MUST GO BACK TO SEE MY MOTHER! WE CANNOT LET ALL THE MORTALS DIE FOR OUR LOVE.

PROMISE ME YOU WILL *RETURN!*

PLEASE.

IF I GO BACK, WILL MOTHER EVER LET ME RETURN? SHE CAN'T STOP ME! I'M A WOMAN NOW.

HERMES, WILL YOU GRANT US A FEW MOMENTS TO SAY GOOD-BYE?

OF COURSE.

WILL YOU WALK WITH ME IN THE ELYSIAN FIELDS, MY LOVE?

YES, MY KING.

I HOPE THIS WON'T BE FOR THE LAST TIME.

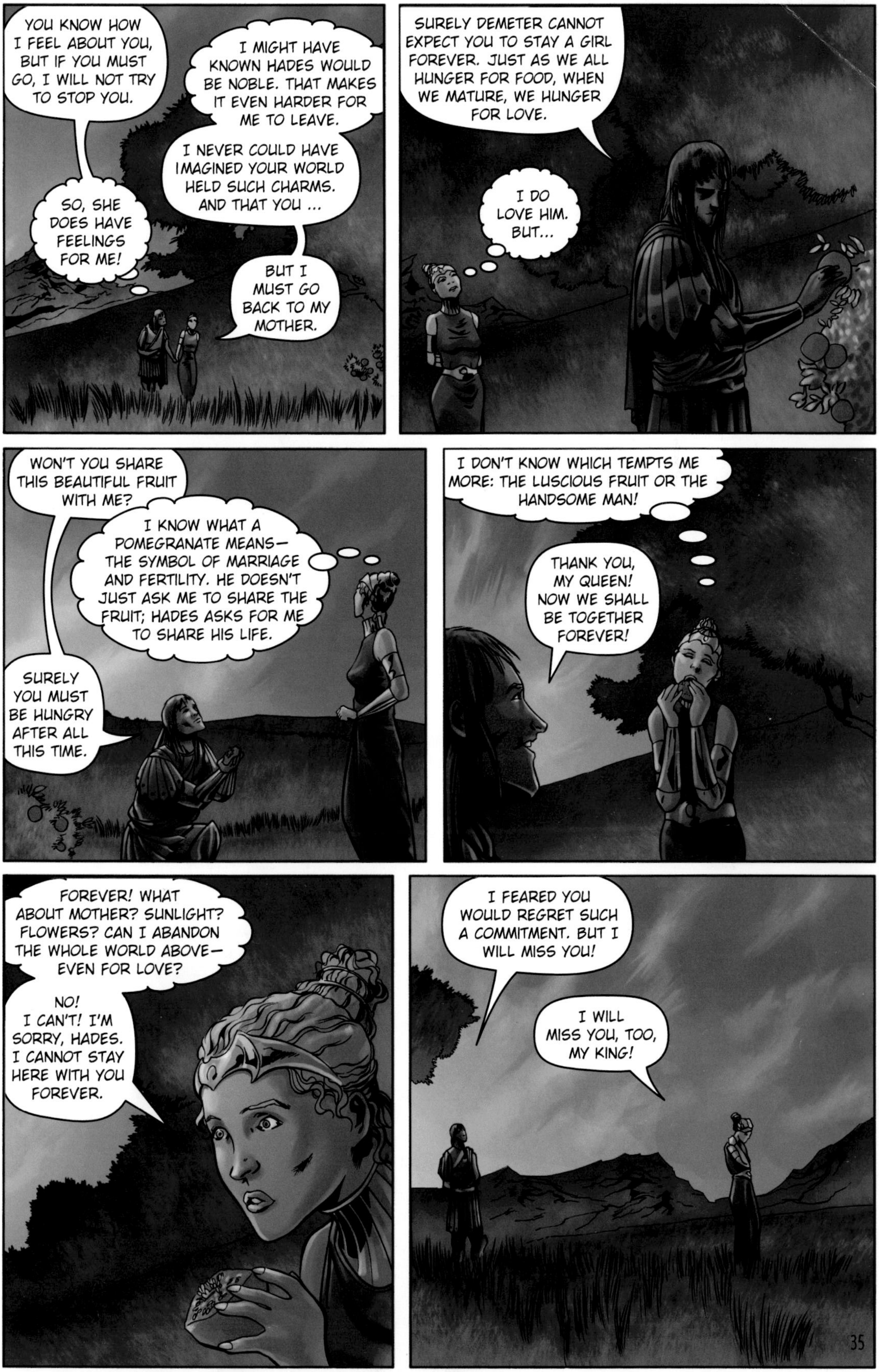
YOU KNOW HOW I FEEL ABOUT YOU, BUT IF YOU MUST GO, I WILL NOT TRY TO STOP YOU.
I MIGHT HAVE KNOWN HADES WOULD BE NOBLE. THAT MAKES IT EVEN HARDER FOR ME TO LEAVE.
I NEVER COULD HAVE IMAGINED YOUR WORLD HELD SUCH CHARMS. AND THAT YOU ...
SO, SHE DOES HAVE FEELINGS FOR ME!
BUT I MUST GO BACK TO MY MOTHER.
SURELY DEMETER CANNOT EXPECT YOU TO STAY A GIRL FOREVER. JUST AS WE ALL HUNGER FOR FOOD, WHEN WE MATURE, WE HUNGER FOR LOVE.
I DO LOVE HIM. BUT...
WON'T YOU SHARE THIS BEAUTIFUL FRUIT WITH ME?
I KNOW WHAT A POMEGRANATE MEANS—THE SYMBOL OF MARRIAGE AND FERTILITY. HE DOESN'T JUST ASK ME TO SHARE THE FRUIT; HADES ASKS FOR ME TO SHARE HIS LIFE.
SURELY YOU MUST BE HUNGRY AFTER ALL THIS TIME.
I DON'T KNOW WHICH TEMPTS ME MORE: THE LUSCIOUS FRUIT OR THE HANDSOME MAN!
THANK YOU, MY QUEEN! NOW WE SHALL BE TOGETHER FOREVER!
FOREVER! WHAT ABOUT MOTHER? SUNLIGHT? FLOWERS? CAN I ABANDON THE WHOLE WORLD ABOVE—EVEN FOR LOVE?
NO! I CAN'T! I'M SORRY, HADES. I CANNOT STAY HERE WITH YOU FOREVER.
I FEARED YOU WOULD REGRET SUCH A COMMITMENT. BUT I WILL MISS YOU!
I WILL MISS YOU, TOO, MY KING!

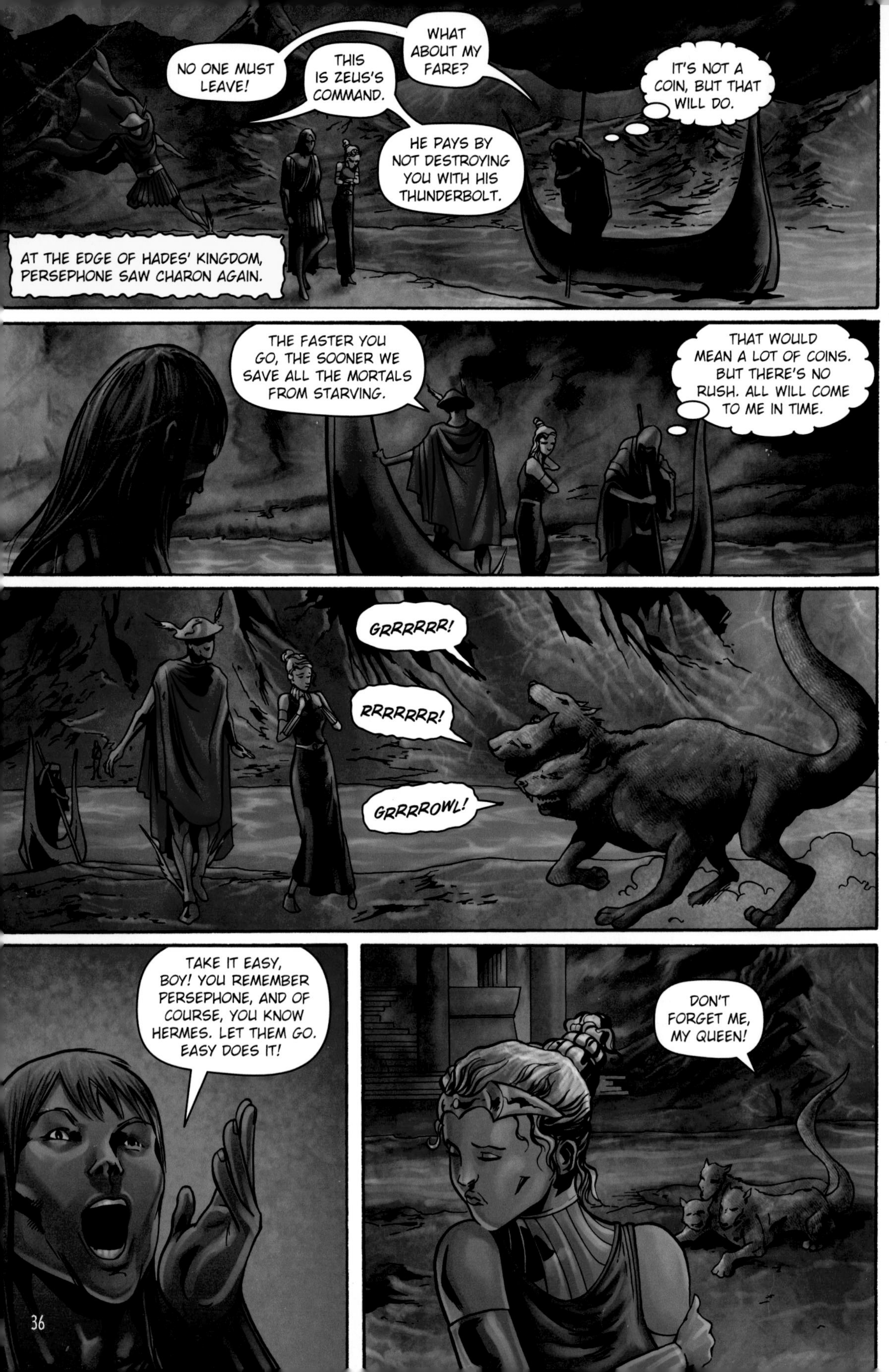
NO ONE MUST LEAVE!
THIS IS ZEUS'S COMMAND.
WHAT ABOUT MY FARE?
HE PAYS BY NOT DESTROYING YOU WITH HIS THUNDERBOLT.
IT'S NOT A COIN, BUT THAT WILL DO.
AT THE EDGE OF HADES' KINGDOM, PERSEPHONE SAW CHARON AGAIN.
THE FASTER YOU GO, THE SOONER WE SAVE ALL THE MORTALS FROM STARVING.
THAT WOULD MEAN A LOT OF COINS. BUT THERE'S NO RUSH. ALL WILL COME TO ME IN TIME.
GRRRRRR!
RRRRRRR!
GRRRROWL!
TAKE IT EASY, BOY! YOU REMEMBER PERSEPHONE, AND OF COURSE, YOU KNOW HERMES. LET THEM GO. EASY DOES IT!
DON'T FORGET ME, MY QUEEN!

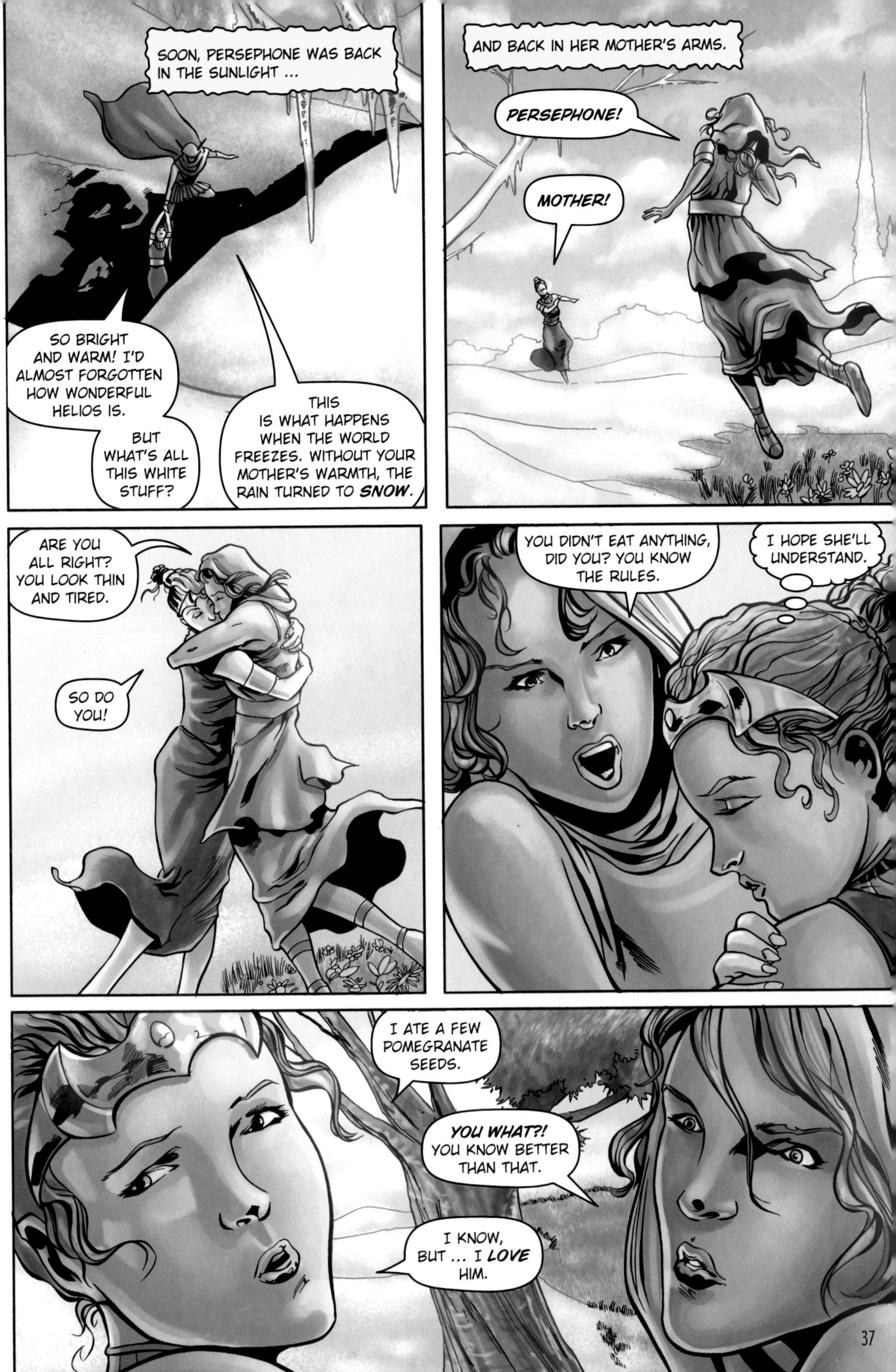
SOON, PERSEPHONE WAS BACK IN THE SUNLIGHT ...
SO BRIGHT AND WARM! I'D ALMOST FORGOTTEN HOW WONDERFUL HELIOS IS.
BUT WHAT'S ALL THIS WHITE STUFF?
THIS IS WHAT HAPPENS WHEN THE WORLD FREEZES. WITHOUT YOUR MOTHER'S WARMTH, THE RAIN TURNED TO **SNOW**.
AND BACK IN HER MOTHER'S ARMS.
PERSEPHONE!
MOTHER!
ARE YOU ALL RIGHT? YOU LOOK THIN AND TIRED.
SO DO YOU!
YOU DIDN'T EAT ANYTHING, DID YOU? YOU KNOW THE RULES.
I HOPE SHE'LL UNDERSTAND.
I ATE A FEW POMEGRANATE SEEDS.
YOU WHAT?! YOU KNOW BETTER THAN THAT.
I KNOW, BUT ... I **LOVE** HIM.

THE POMEGRANATE PROBLEM

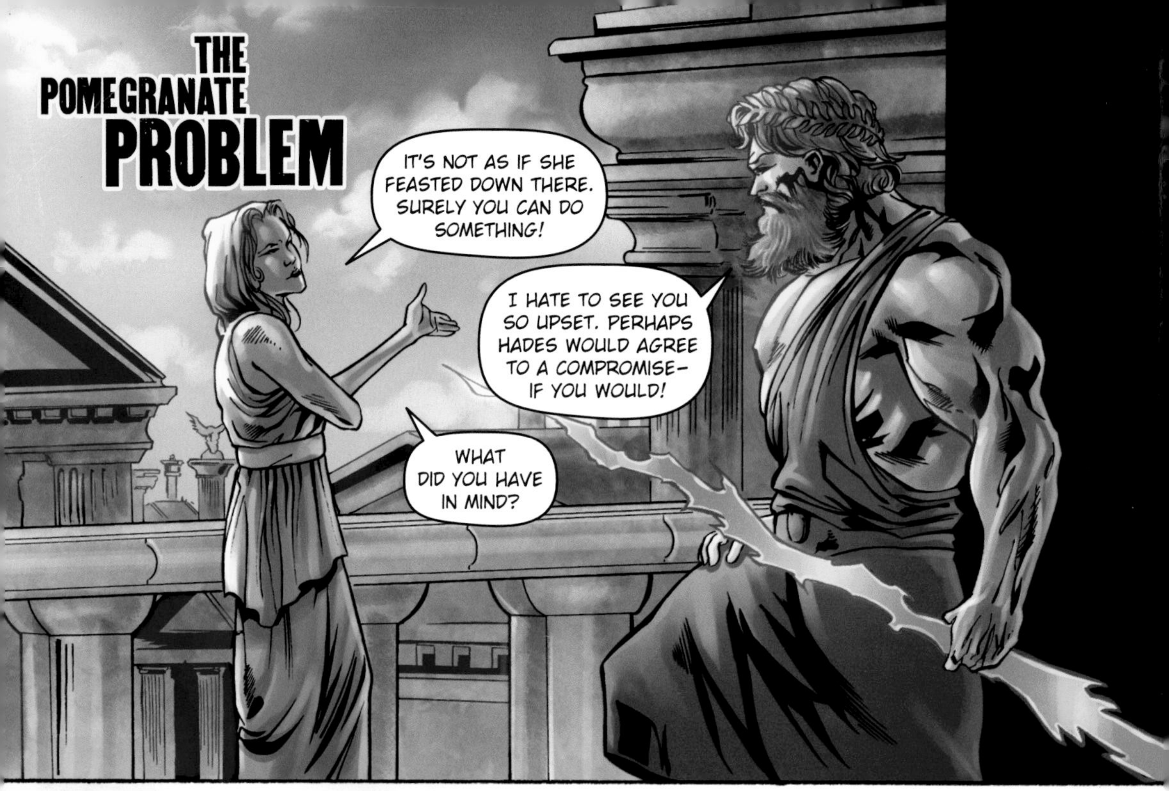
IT'S NOT AS IF SHE FEASTED DOWN THERE. SURELY YOU CAN DO SOMETHING!
I HATE TO SEE YOU SO UPSET. PERHAPS HADES WOULD AGREE TO A COMPROMISE–IF YOU WOULD!
WHAT DID YOU HAVE IN MIND?

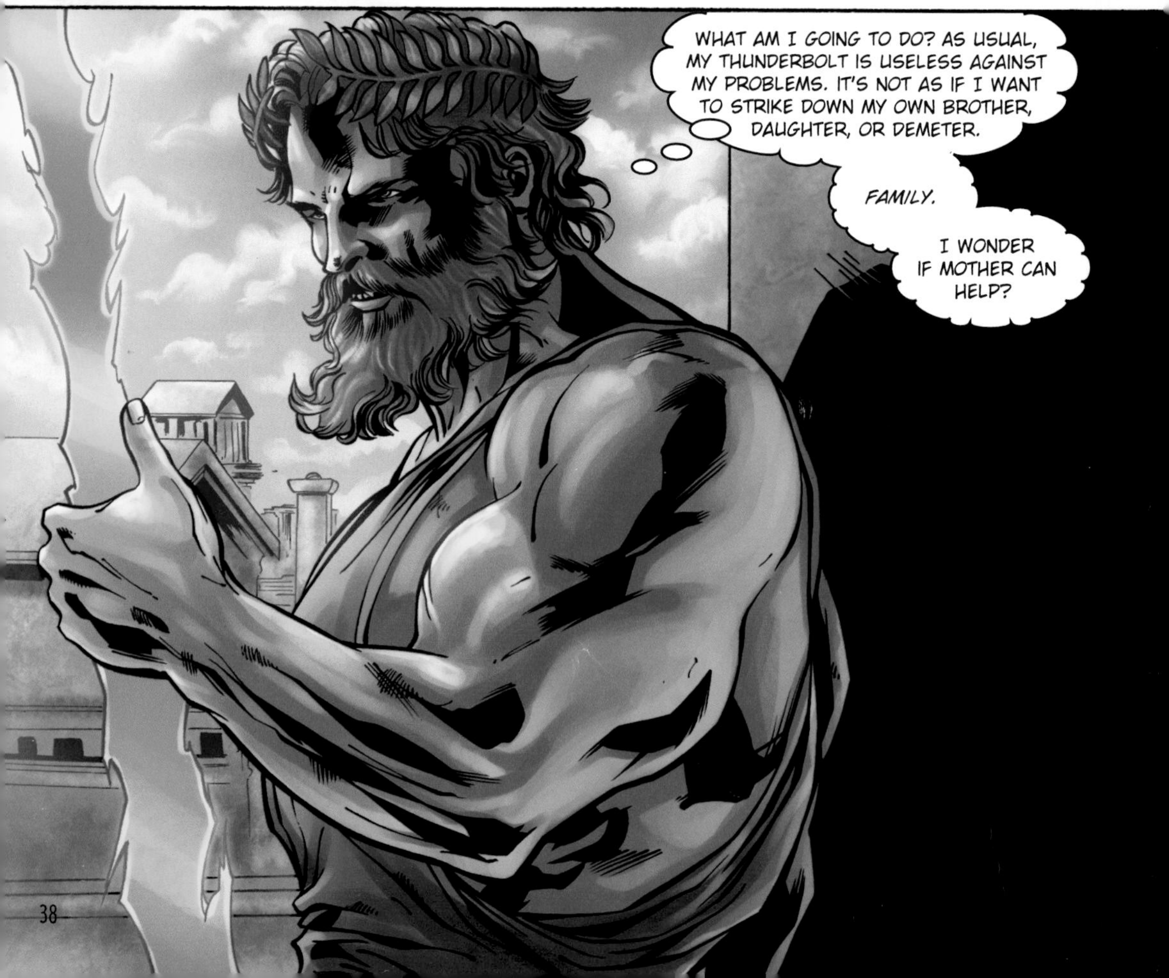
WHAT AM I GOING TO DO? AS USUAL, MY THUNDERBOLT IS USELESS AGAINST MY PROBLEMS. IT'S NOT AS IF I WANT TO STRIKE DOWN MY OWN BROTHER, DAUGHTER, OR DEMETER.
FAMILY.
I WONDER IF MOTHER CAN HELP?

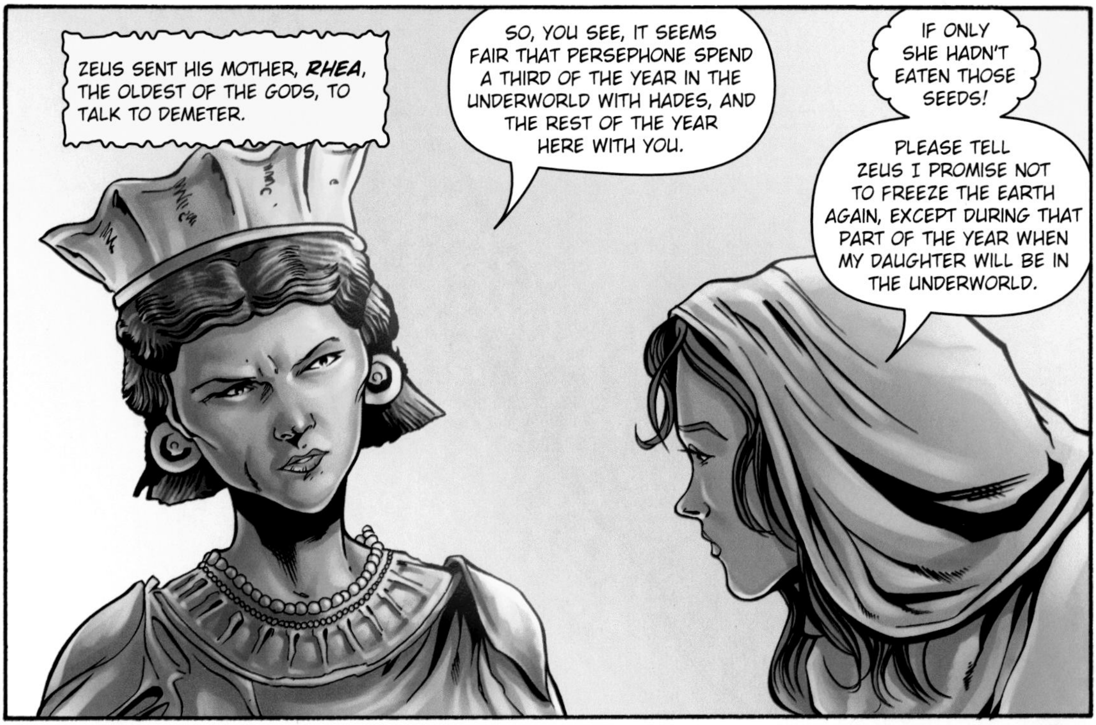
ZEUS SENT HIS MOTHER, **RHEA**, THE OLDEST OF THE GODS, TO TALK TO DEMETER.
SO, YOU SEE, IT SEEMS FAIR THAT PERSEPHONE SPEND A THIRD OF THE YEAR IN THE UNDERWORLD WITH HADES, AND THE REST OF THE YEAR HERE WITH YOU.
IF ONLY SHE HADN'T EATEN THOSE SEEDS!
PLEASE TELL ZEUS I PROMISE NOT TO FREEZE THE EARTH AGAIN, EXCEPT DURING THAT PART OF THE YEAR WHEN MY DAUGHTER WILL BE IN THE UNDERWORLD.

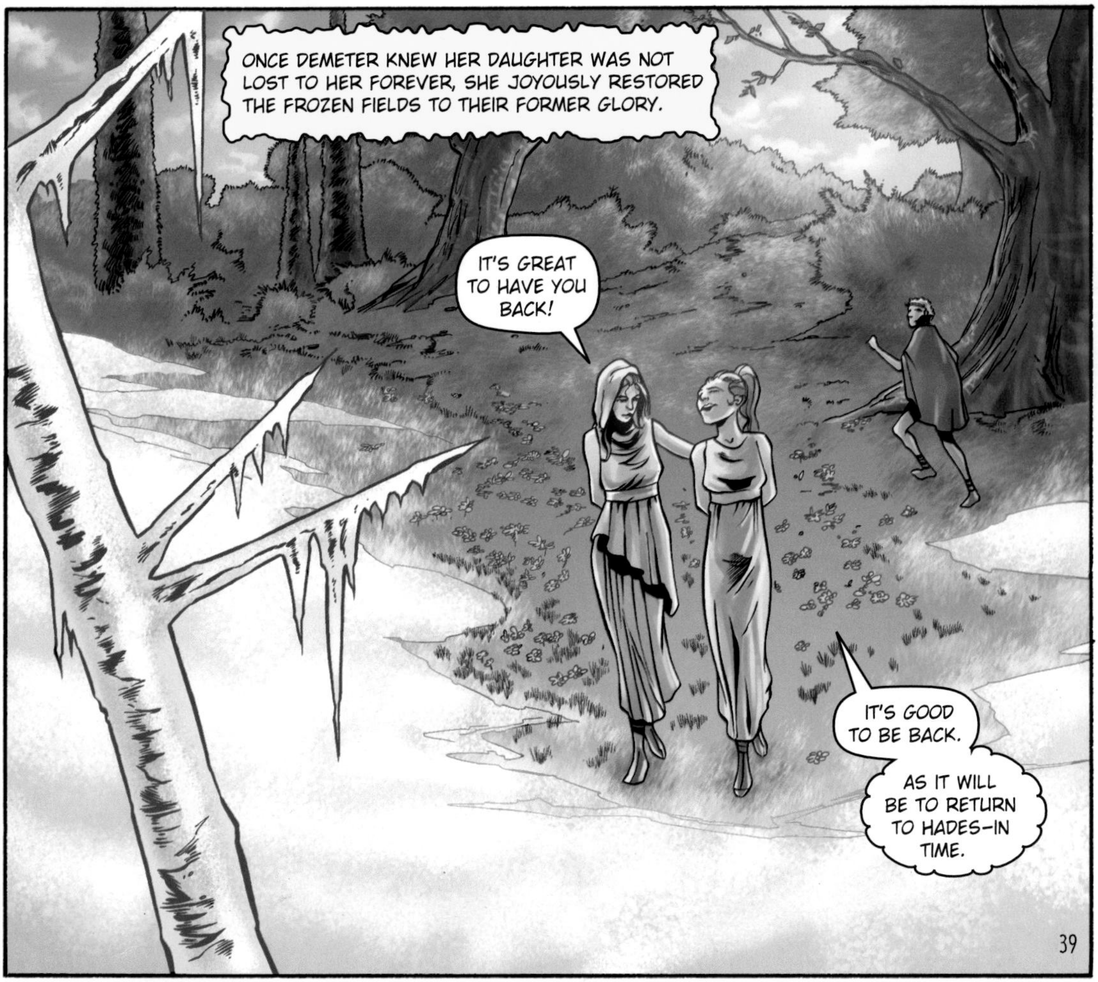
ONCE DEMETER KNEW HER DAUGHTER WAS NOT LOST TO HER FOREVER, SHE JOYOUSLY RESTORED THE FROZEN FIELDS TO THEIR FORMER GLORY.
IT'S GREAT TO HAVE YOU BACK!
IT'S GOOD TO BE BACK.
AS IT WILL BE TO RETURN TO HADES–IN TIME.

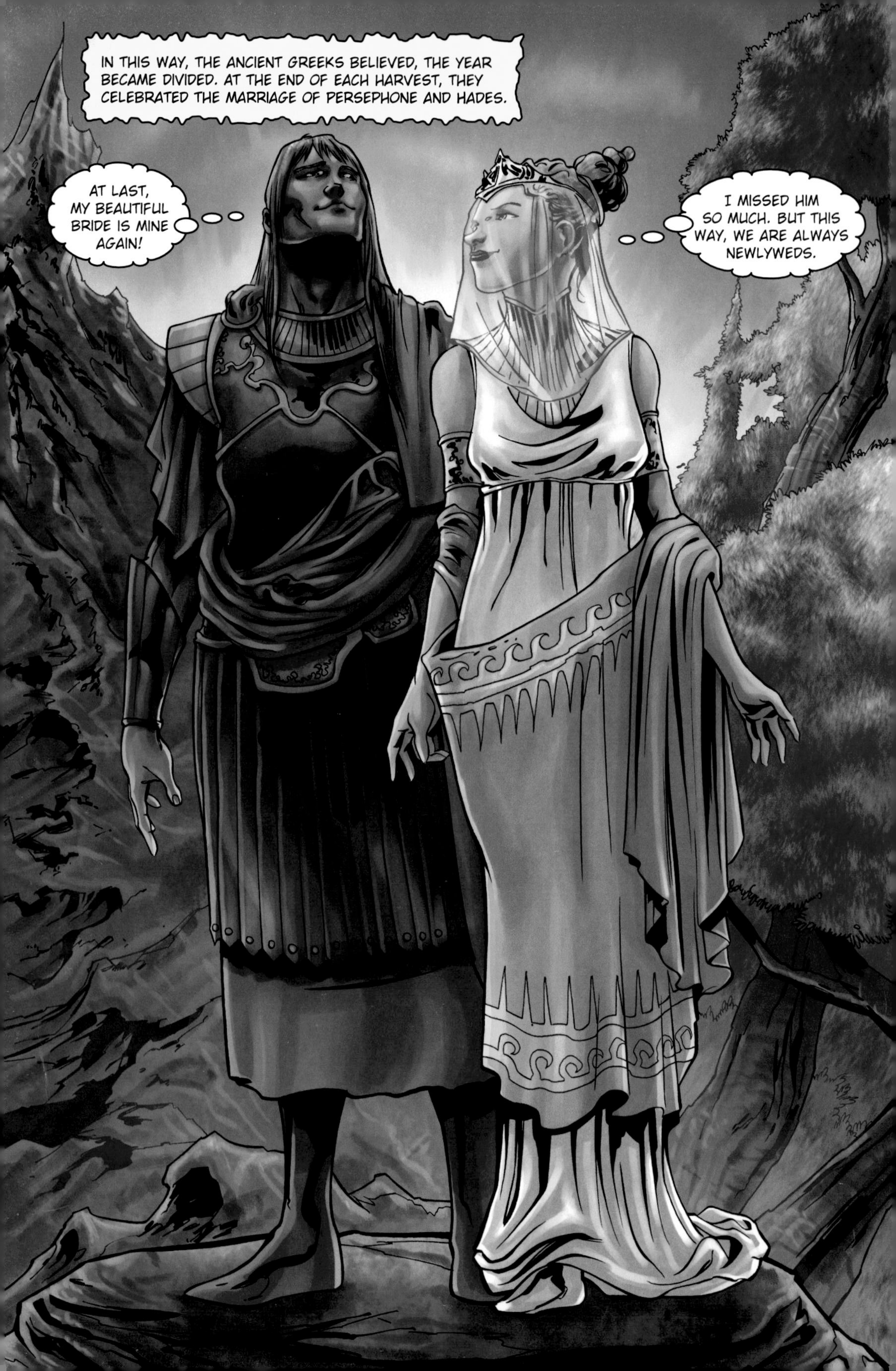
IN THIS WAY, THE ANCIENT GREEKS BELIEVED, THE YEAR BECAME DIVIDED. AT THE END OF EACH HARVEST, THEY CELEBRATED THE MARRIAGE OF PERSEPHONE AND HADES.
AT LAST, MY BEAUTIFUL BRIDE IS MINE AGAIN!
I MISSED HIM SO MUCH. BUT THIS WAY, WE ARE ALWAYS NEWLYWEDS.

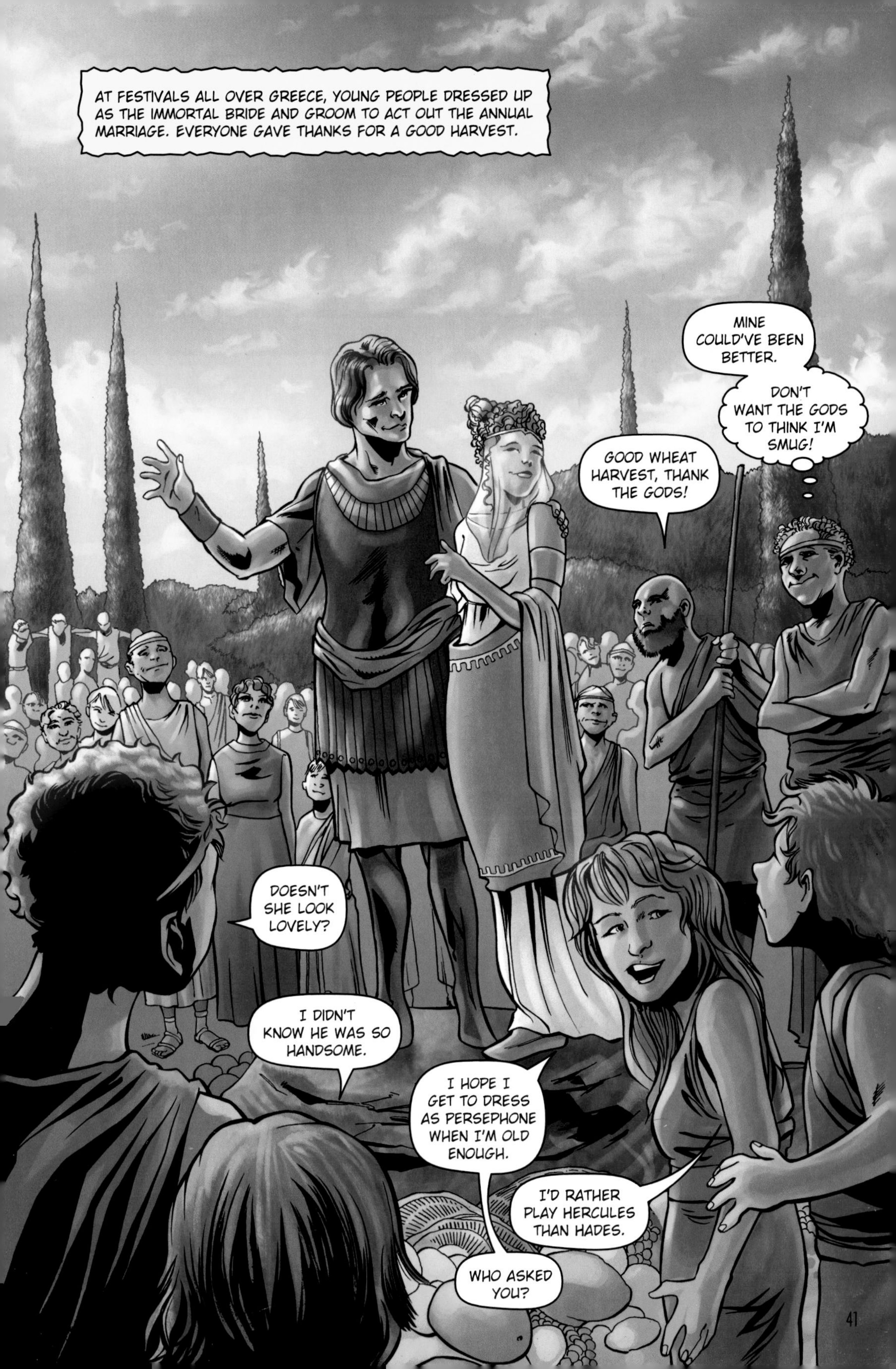

AT FESTIVALS ALL OVER GREECE, YOUNG PEOPLE DRESSED UP AS THE IMMORTAL BRIDE AND GROOM TO ACT OUT THE ANNUAL MARRIAGE. EVERYONE GAVE THANKS FOR A GOOD HARVEST.
GOOD WHEAT HARVEST, THANK THE GODS!
MINE COULD'VE BEEN BETTER.
DON'T WANT THE GODS TO THINK I'M SMUG!
DOESN'T SHE LOOK LOVELY?
I DIDN'T KNOW HE WAS SO HANDSOME.
I HOPE I GET TO DRESS AS PERSEPHONE WHEN I'M OLD ENOUGH.
I'D RATHER PLAY HERCULES THAN HADES.
WHO ASKED YOU?

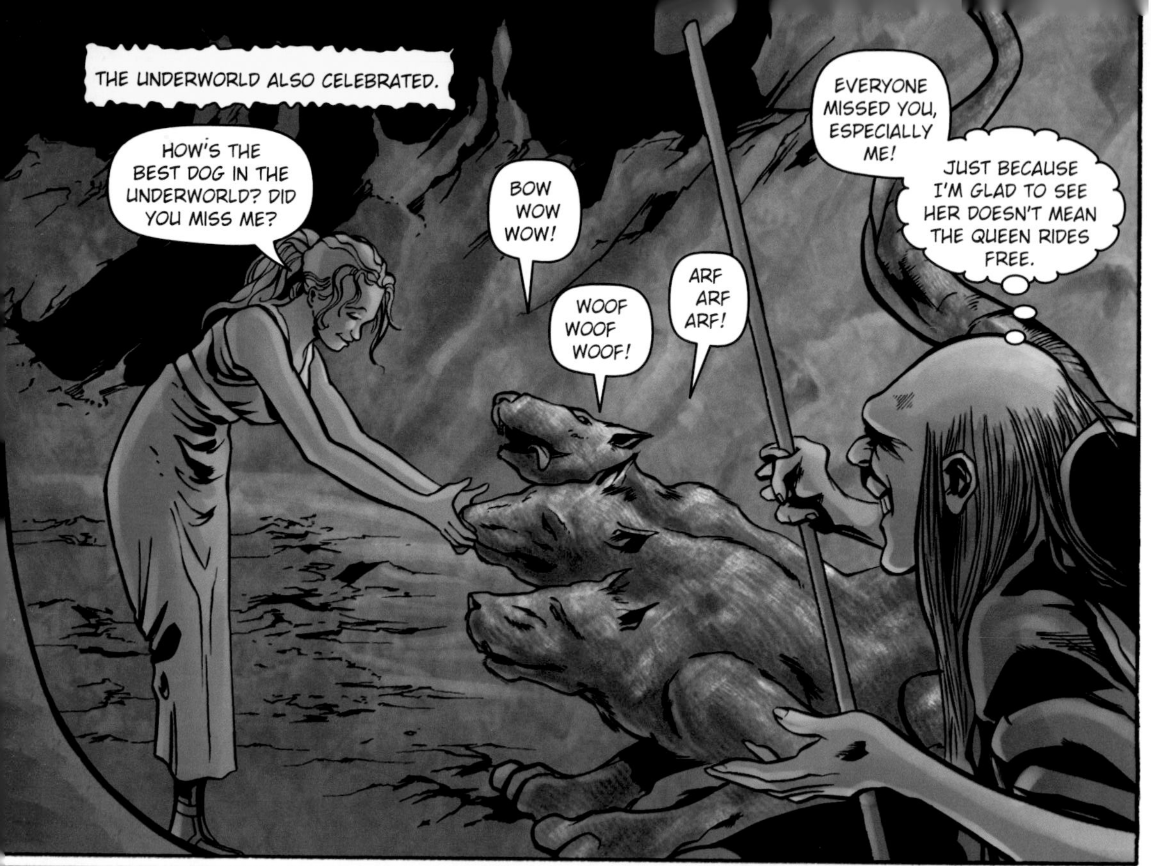
THE UNDERWORLD ALSO CELEBRATED.
HOW'S THE BEST DOG IN THE UNDERWORLD? DID YOU MISS ME?
BOW WOW WOW!
WOOF WOOF WOOF!
ARF ARF ARF!
EVERYONE MISSED YOU, ESPECIALLY ME!
JUST BECAUSE I'M GLAD TO SEE HER DOESN'T MEAN THE QUEEN RIDES FREE.

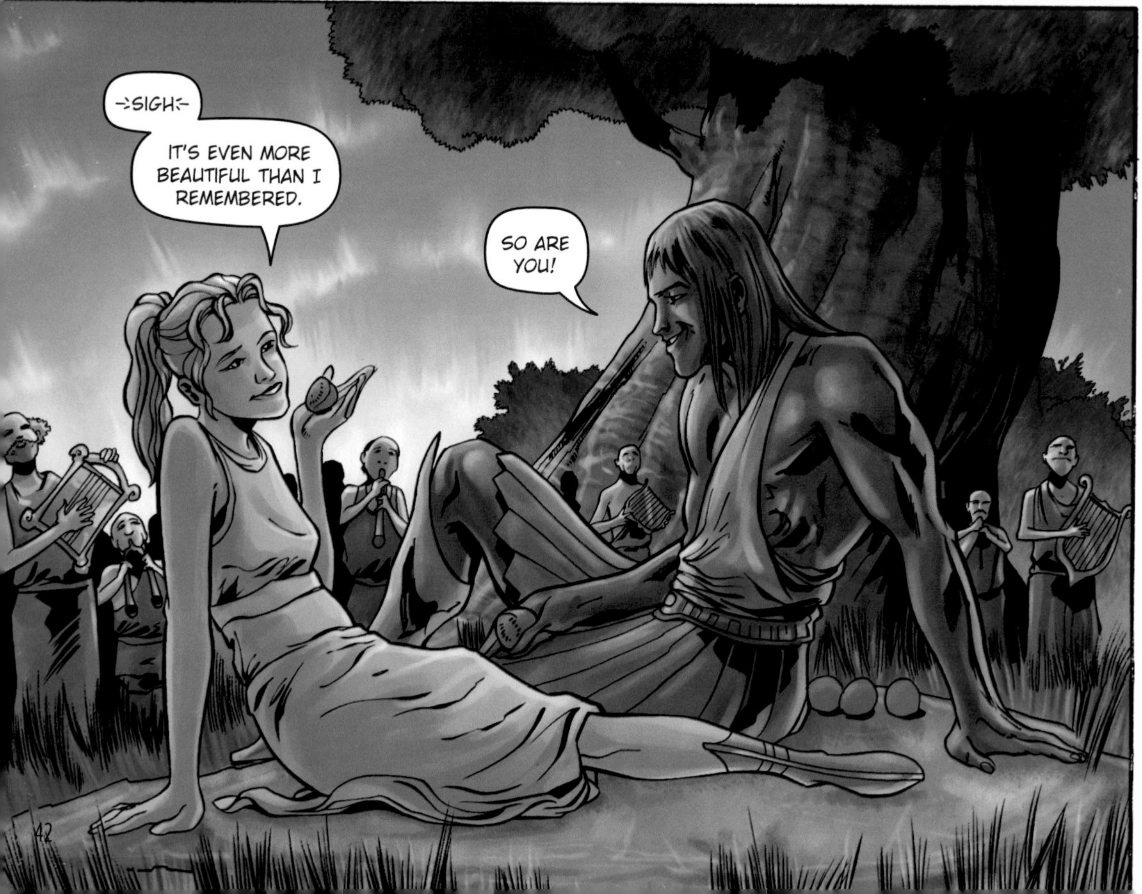
SIGH
IT'S EVEN MORE BEAUTIFUL THAN I REMEMBERED.
SO ARE YOU!

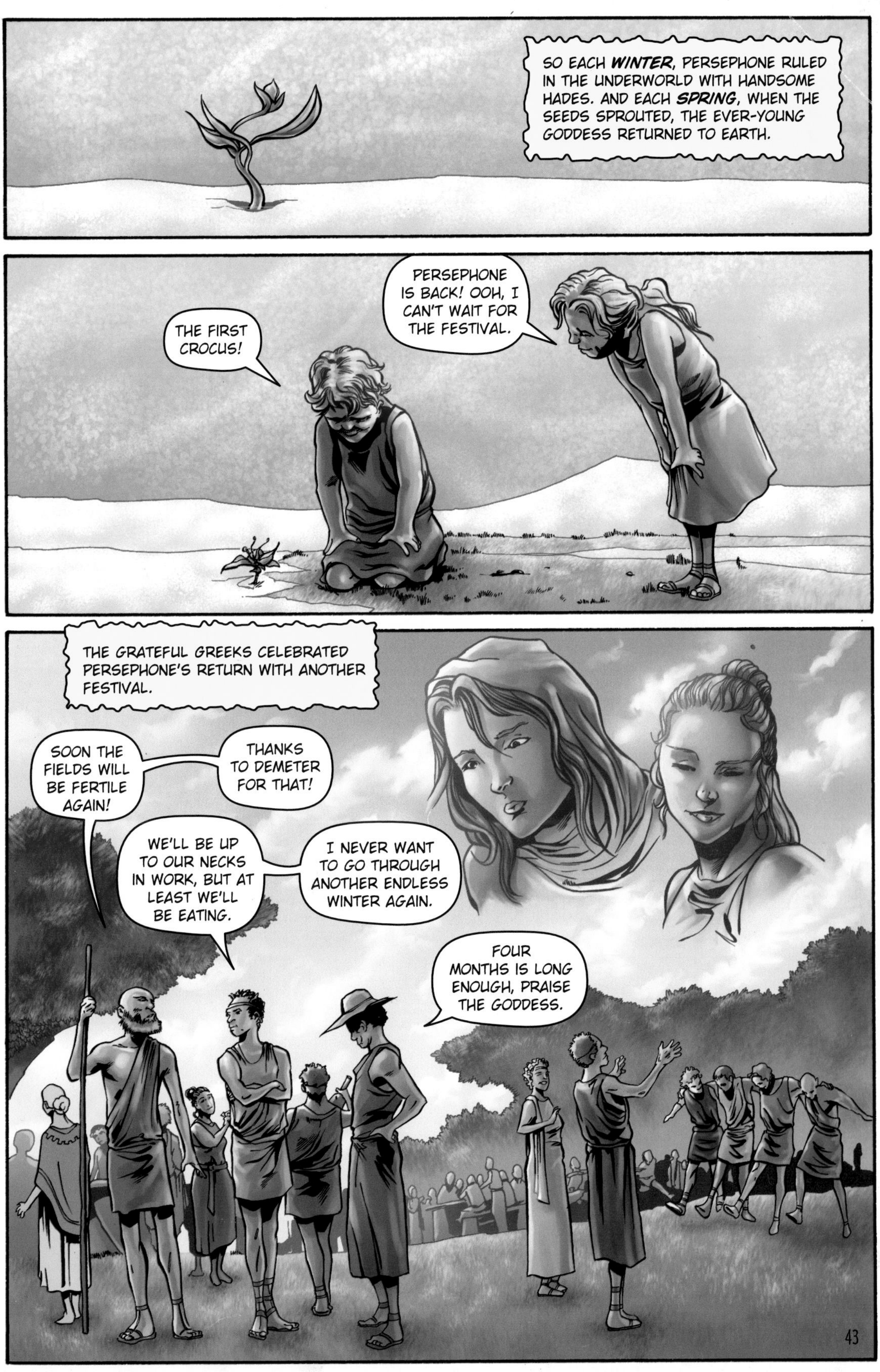
SO EACH ***WINTER***, PERSEPHONE RULED IN THE UNDERWORLD WITH HANDSOME HADES. AND EACH ***SPRING***, WHEN THE SEEDS SPROUTED, THE EVER-YOUNG GODDESS RETURNED TO EARTH.
THE FIRST CROCUS!
PERSEPHONE IS BACK! OOH, I CAN'T WAIT FOR THE FESTIVAL.
THE GRATEFUL GREEKS CELEBRATED PERSEPHONE'S RETURN WITH ANOTHER FESTIVAL.
SOON THE FIELDS WILL BE FERTILE AGAIN!
THANKS TO DEMETER FOR THAT!
WE'LL BE UP TO OUR NECKS IN WORK, BUT AT LEAST WE'LL BE EATING.
I NEVER WANT TO GO THROUGH ANOTHER ENDLESS WINTER AGAIN.
FOUR MONTHS IS LONG ENOUGH, PRAISE THE GODDESS.

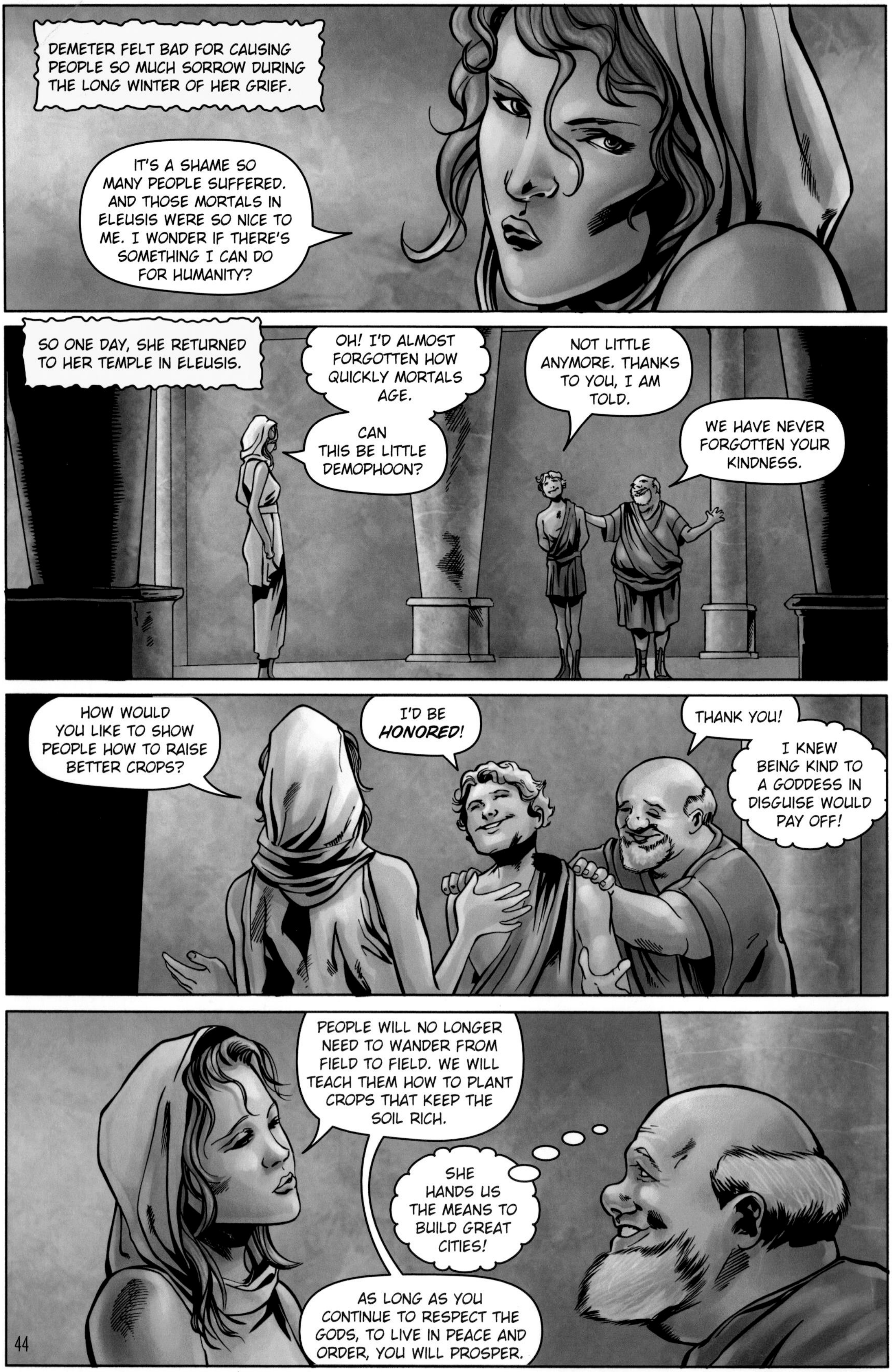
DEMETER FELT BAD FOR CAUSING PEOPLE SO MUCH SORROW DURING THE LONG WINTER OF HER GRIEF.
IT'S A SHAME SO MANY PEOPLE SUFFERED. AND THOSE MORTALS IN ELEUSIS WERE SO NICE TO ME. I WONDER IF THERE'S SOMETHING I CAN DO FOR HUMANITY?
SO ONE DAY, SHE RETURNED TO HER TEMPLE IN ELEUSIS.
OH! I'D ALMOST FORGOTTEN HOW QUICKLY MORTALS AGE.
CAN THIS BE LITTLE DEMOPHOON?
NOT LITTLE ANYMORE. THANKS TO YOU, I AM TOLD.
WE HAVE NEVER FORGOTTEN YOUR KINDNESS.
HOW WOULD YOU LIKE TO SHOW PEOPLE HOW TO RAISE BETTER CROPS?
I'D BE *HONORED*!
THANK YOU!
I KNEW BEING KIND TO A GODDESS IN DISGUISE WOULD PAY OFF!
PEOPLE WILL NO LONGER NEED TO WANDER FROM FIELD TO FIELD. WE WILL TEACH THEM HOW TO PLANT CROPS THAT KEEP THE SOIL RICH.
SHE HANDS US THE MEANS TO BUILD GREAT CITIES!
AS LONG AS YOU CONTINUE TO RESPECT THE GODS, TO LIVE IN PEACE AND ORDER, YOU WILL PROSPER.

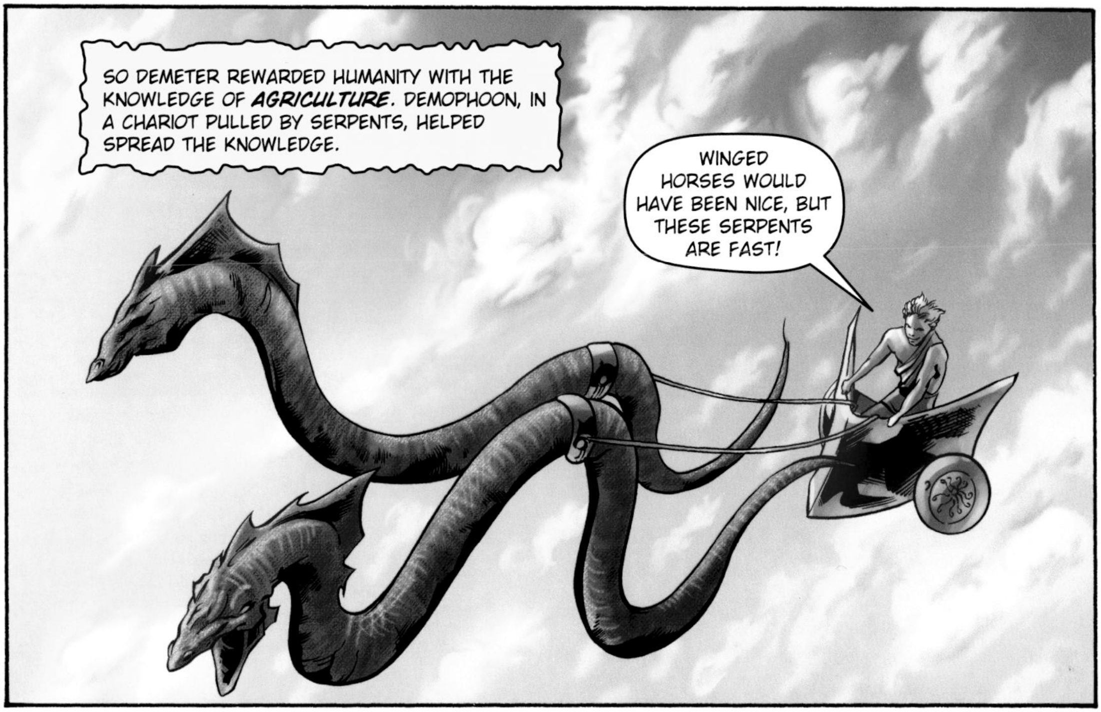
SO DEMETER REWARDED HUMANITY WITH THE KNOWLEDGE OF ***AGRICULTURE***. DEMOPHOON, IN A CHARIOT PULLED BY SERPENTS, HELPED SPREAD THE KNOWLEDGE.
WINGED HORSES WOULD HAVE BEEN NICE, BUT THESE SERPENTS ARE FAST!

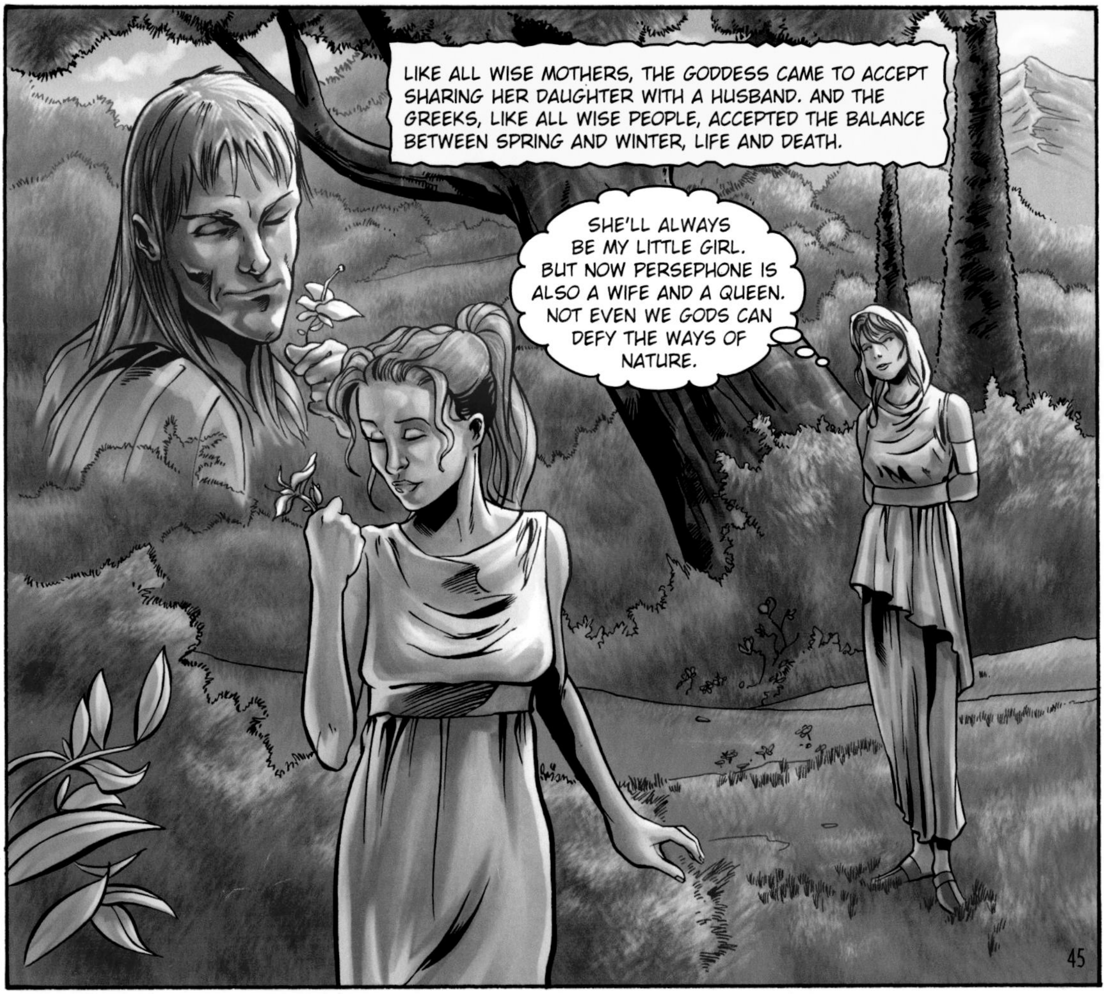
LIKE ALL WISE MOTHERS, THE GODDESS CAME TO ACCEPT SHARING HER DAUGHTER WITH A HUSBAND. AND THE GREEKS, LIKE ALL WISE PEOPLE, ACCEPTED THE BALANCE BETWEEN SPRING AND WINTER, LIFE AND DEATH.
SHE'LL ALWAYS BE MY LITTLE GIRL. BUT NOW PERSEPHONE IS ALSO A WIFE AND A QUEEN. NOT EVEN WE GODS CAN DEFY THE WAYS OF NATURE.

GLOSSARY AND PRONUNCIATION GUIDE

AMBROSIA (am-*broh*-zhuh): the food of the gods, made from divine substances. Humans sometimes made their own imitation ambrosia from honey, water, fruit, cheese, olive oil, and barley (a grain).

APHRODITE (a-*froh*-dye-tee): the Greek goddess of love

ARES (*air*-eez): the Greek god of war

ATHENA (*uh*-thee-nuh): the Greek goddess of wisdom

CHARON (*kair*-ahn): the boatman who guides souls across the river Styx into the underworld

DEMETER (*dim*-eh-tur): the Greek goddess of the harvest and of agriculture

DEMOPHOON (deh-*mah*-foh-awn): the son of King Celeus and Queen Metaneira of Eleusis, taken care of as a child by Demeter

ELEUSIS (ih-*loo*-sis): a city in Greece northwest of Athens, center of the Eleusinian mysteries—sacred festivals dedicated to Demeter

ELYSIAN FIELDS (ih-*lee*-zhun): a beautiful part of the underworld where heroes and poets are sent after death

FURIES: the three female spirits, Tisiphone, Megara, and Allecto, of justice and vengeance. Also known as the Erinyes, their job is to pursue wrongdoers.

HADES (*hay*-deez): the Greek god of the underworld

HERA (*hehr*-uh): the Greek goddess of marriage and childbirth, married to Zeus

HERMES (*hur*-meez): the messenger of the gods on Mount Olympus

MOUNT OLYMPUS: the home of the Greek gods and goddesses

PERSEPHONE (per-*sef*-uh-nee): Demeter's daughter, kidnapped by Hades

SHADES: the spirits of dead people who inhabit the underworld

STYX (stiks): the river that encircles the underworld. Once shades are ferried across the Styx by Charon, they cannot return to the world above.

UNDERWORLD: the kingdom of the dead, ruled by Hades

ZEUS (zoos): the main Greek god, the ruler of Mount Olympus

FURTHER READING AND WEBSITES

Bolton, Lesley. *The Everything Classical Mythology Book: Greek and Roman Gods, Goddesses, Heroes, and Monsters from Ares to Zeus*. Avon, MA: Adams Media Corporation, 2002. This who's who guide introduces young readers to Greek and Roman mythology.

Day, Nancy. *Your Travel Guide to Ancient Greece*. Minneapolis: Twenty-First Century Books, 2001. Day prepares readers for a trip back to ancient Greece, including which cities to visit, how to get around, what to wear, and how to fit in with the locals.

Hamilton, Edith. *Mythology*. Boston: Little, Brown & Co., 1942. Hamilton's classic book focuses on the stories of Greek gods and heroes, but it also covers Roman and Norse myths.

Macdonald, Fiona. *Gods and Goddesses in the Daily Life of the Ancient Greeks*. New York: Peter Bedrick Books, 2001. Macdonald provides an introduction to the traditions and religious beliefs of the ancient Greeks, with photographs, illustrations, and detailed diagrams.

MythWeb. http://www.mythweb.com/index.html. This site, with a searchable encyclopedia, provides students with information on gods, goddesses, and places in Greek myth.

CREATING *DEMETER & PERSEPHONE*

In retelling this ancient story for modern readers, Justine and Ron Fontes drew upon classical and modern sources such as *Metamorphoses* by the Roman poet Ovid (43 B.C.–ca. A.D. 17), Edith Hamilton's *Mythology*, and the *New Larousse Encyclopedia of Mythology*. Artist Steve Kurth used classical Greek art, such as painted vases and stone carvings, and anthropological sources to create the story's visual details. David Mulroy of the University of Wisconsin-Milwaukee ensured historical and visual accuracy.

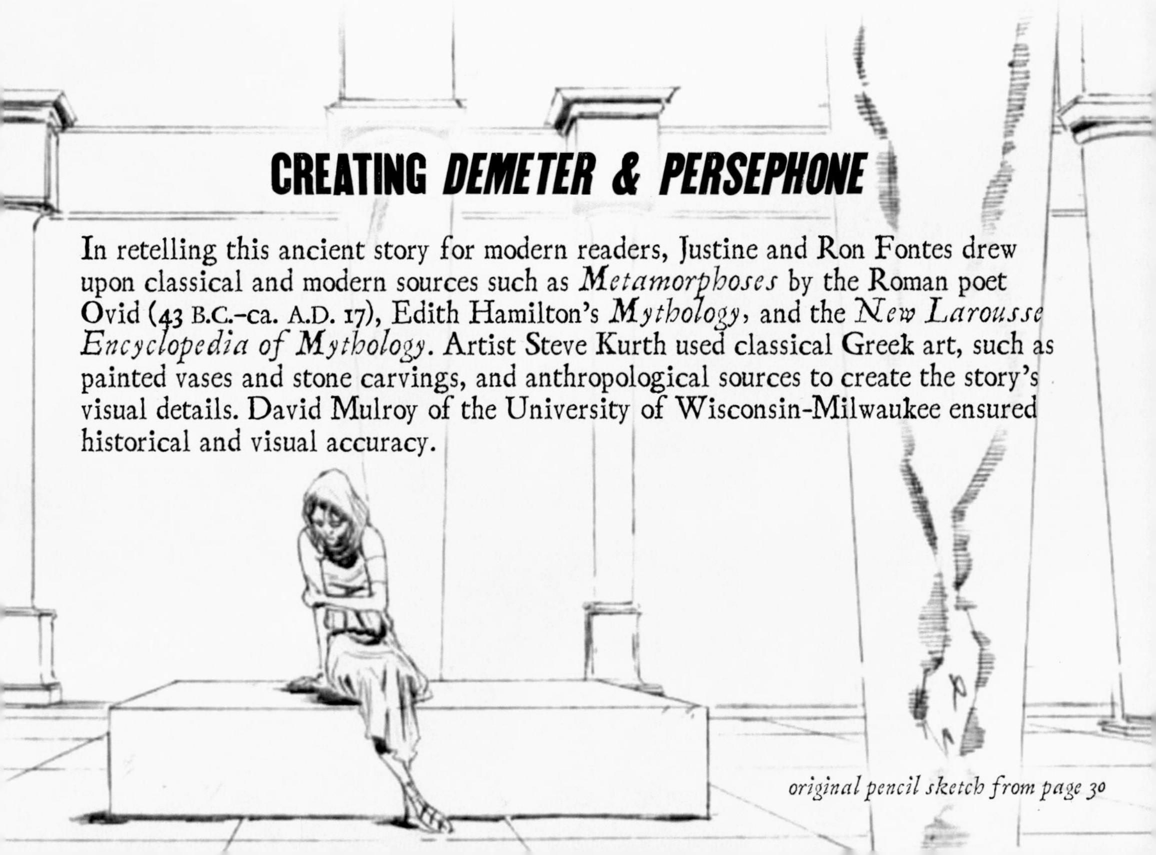

original pencil sketch from page 30

INDEX

ABOUT THE AUTHORS AND THE ARTIST

JUSTINE AND RON FONTES met at a publishing house in New York City, where Ron worked in the comic book department and Justine was an editorial assistant in children's books. Together they have written nearly 500 children's books, in every format from board books to historical novels. From their home in Maine, they also launched Sonic Comics with their first graphic novel *Tales of the Terminal Diner*. Other published projects include *The Trojan Horse: The Fall of Troy*, *Atalanta: The Race against Destiny*, and *The Wooden Sword*. Lifelong library lovers, the Fonteses long to write 1,001 books before retiring to read.

STEVE KURTH was born and raised in west central Wisconsin. He graduated with a BFA in illustration from the University of Wisconsin-Eau Claire. Steve's art has appeared in *Hercules: The Twelve Labors* and in numerous comic books, including *G.I. Joe*, *Micronauts*, *Ghostbusters*, *Dragonlance*, and *Cracked* magazine.